homestyle quilts

simple patterns *and* savory recipes

Kim Diehl *and* Laurie Baker

Martingale®
Create with Confidence

Homestyle Quilts: Simple Patterns and Savory Recipes
© 2012 by Kim Diehl and Laurie Baker

Martingale®
19021 120th Ave. NE, Ste. 102
Bothell, WA 98011-9511 USA
ShopMartingale.com

Printed in China
17 16 15 14 13 12   8 7 6 5 4 3 2 1

Library of Congress Cataloging-in-Publication Data is available upon request.

ISBN: 978-1-60468-163-5

MISSION STATEMENT

Dedicated to providing quality products and service to inspire creativity.

CREDITS

President & CEO: Tom Wierzbicki
Editor in Chief: Mary V. Green
Design Director: Paula Schlosser
Managing Editor: Karen Costello Soltys
Technical Editor: Nancy Mahoney
Copy Editor: Melissa Bryan
Production Manager: Regina Girard
Illustrator: Missy Shepler
Cover & Text Designer: Regina Girard
Photographer: Brent Kane

Martingale thanks Bank of Bargains, located on Main Street in Bothell, Washington, for graciously lending the vintage Hotpoint stove shown on pages 6 and 65.

Special thanks also to Karen and Casey Burns of Carnation, Washington, for allowing us to photograph in their home.

dedication

To my many quilting friends both near and far who share my love of cutting up perfectly fine fabric and then piecing it all back together again. ~*Kim*

To all the women who infused my childhood with their talents and helped shape my creative spirit: my mom, Jeanne Edwards, for being the ultimate domestic role model and teaching me to sew, stitch, cook, and garden; my great-aunt, Kathryn Smithers, for showing me that fun and creativity have no age limit; and Mrs. Thecla Aaron and Mrs. Minnie Graham, the two neighbors I was blessed to live between when growing up, who taught me just about every needle art and craft possible. And to Margaret Noe, who's been waiting 30 years for me to cross off "write a book" from my bucket list. ~*Laurie*

acknowledgments

Kim would like to thank:

Barbara Walsh for her impeccable workmanship and patchwork skills in helping piece the "Plain Jane" quilt.

Deborah Poole for sharing her amazing artistic abilities through the machine quilting of the projects shared in this book.

Jo Morton for keeping me well stocked with her many beautiful fabrics that continually find their way into my quilts.

Janome America for the use of their incomparable Memory Craft 11000 sewing machine.

Laurie would like to thank:

Kim Diehl for including me in this designing and writing adventure. I couldn't think of a better traveling companion.

Sherrie Coppenbarger for taking on the task of machine quilting all of my projects and helping me work through the details.

Konnie Arnemann for binding "Four Patch Potpourri," "Paint the Sky," and "Garden Ambrosia."

My family for their patience in dealing with the fiber explosions that seemed to take over every room in the house while I was trying to find just the right fabric.

contents

Introduction 7

Bygone Baskets 8
    Santa Fe Soup 13
Easy Peasy 14
    Peppered Bacon and Clam Chowder 19
Roundabout Crisscross 20
    Chicken Tostadas 25
Blackbirds and Berries 26
    Chicken Pot Pie 31
Four Patch Potpourri 34
    Pizza Casserole 39
Plain Jane 42
    Kim's Favorite Meat Loaf 47
Paint the Sky 48
    Beef Stroganoff 53
Farmhouse Furrows 54
    Slow Cooker BBQ Beef Sandwiches 59
Penny Pincher 60
    Easy Pot Roast 63
Prairie Star Posies 64
    Seafood Stuffed Tomatoes 69
Garden Ambrosia 70
    Stuffed Green Peppers 75
Crossing Paths 76
    Easiest Chicken Dinner Ever 79
Cozy Home Lane 80
    Rhubarb Blueberry Crisp 85

Quiltmaking Basics 86
About the Authors 96

introduction

First, we'd like to tell you a little bit about ourselves. "We" are Kim Diehl, an Idaho quilt and fabric designer and the author of Martingale's "Simple" series of quilting books, and Laurie Baker, an editor and writer with more than 20 years of experience in the quilting, sewing, and crafting industries, who lives in Illinois. While working together on Kim's book *Simple Seasons* several years ago, we became more than just colleagues . . . we became fast friends. And although we live more than a thousand miles apart, we remain in touch almost daily, sharing a passion for quiltmaking and a love of delicious meals—especially meals that can be prepared easily without tearing us away from our sewing rooms and busy schedules for long.

Comparing quilting projects and swapping recipes is something we do frequently, and one day as we were visiting, we figuratively put our heads together and realized that there are scads of other quiltmakers who are just like us. We all love gathering up our fabrics and diving into a brand-new quilt project, and we really love quilts that are quick and doable without eating up months of our life. And because we also love delicious meals, but don't have time to spend hours in the kitchen preparing them, we create and search out recipes that are tasty and mouthwatering, especially those that can practically cook themselves. What better way to free up our time so that we can fit more into our busy days?

Our goal as we worked together on this fun book was to create a well-rounded collection of quilts—projects that feature a simple blend of patchwork

and appliqué, but don't sacrifice style, only the long-term commitment needed to make them. And yes, we've found that even quilts containing appliqué can be "quick quilts." Our quilts feature appliqué with gentle shapes and a limited amount of pieces . . . we're quite proud to say we used restraint!

With today's modern piecing techniques and Kim's easy invisible machine appliqué method, any quilt in this collection can be made in about a weekend. This means that you can cut out your pieces and sit down to sew on a Friday afternoon and have a completed quilt top as your Sunday afternoon begins to wind down. Of course, stopping to admire your handiwork or taking numerous chocolate breaks may affect your progress, but we'll leave that entirely up to you.

And while we've seldom met a quiltmaker who doesn't love a good meal after a big day of stitching, we've yet to meet one who wants to spend hours preparing it. So what could be better than turning on the slow cooker or throwing together a quick casserole or soup and letting it fill your home with delicious aromas while you stitch? To help you maximize your sewing time and spend a minimum amount of time cooking, we hope you'll give some of our favorite tried-and-true recipes a whirl. Your family will think you spent hours in the kitchen, and we certainly won't tell!

It's our heartfelt wish that you'll treat yourself to some much-deserved stitching time, some simple but yummy dishes, and a rainbow of beautiful quilts.

~Kim and Laurie

bygone baskets

Bring a bit of your flower garden inside your home with this sweet little quilt. Brimming with old-fashioned flavor, the baskets are enhanced with just a touch of easy appliqué and quick-to-make yo-yos to give this piece that special something extra.

MATERIALS

1⅛ yards of pale-yellow solid for blocks and border
⅝ yard of dark-pink print #1 for blocks and binding
1 fat quarter (18" x 22") of medium-green print #1 for blocks
1 fat quarter of dark-green print for vine and leaf appliqués
1 fat eighth (9" x 22") of medium-pink print #1 for blocks
Scrap of medium-green print #2 for leaf appliqués
Scraps of medium-pink print #2 and dark-pink print #2 for yo-yos
1⅛ yards of fabric for backing
37" x 37" square of batting
Bias bar
Liquid basting glue for fabric
#12 perle cotton in dark pink
Size 5 embroidery needle
4 light-pink ⅝"-diameter buttons

CUTTING

Cut all pieces across the width of the fabric unless otherwise noted. Refer to page 13 for appliqué pattern A and to "Kim's Invisible Machine Appliqué Technique" on page 87 for pattern-piece preparation. Refer to "Cutting Bias Strips" on page 86 to cut bias strips. Refer to page 13 for the yo-yo pattern.

From the pale-yellow solid, cut:
3 strips, 3⅜" x 42"; crosscut into 26 squares, 3⅜" x 3⅜". Cut each
   square in half diagonally *once* to yield 52 triangles.
6 strips, 3" x 42"; crosscut into:
   2 strips, 3" x 30½"
   2 strips, 3" x 25½"
   8 rectangles, 3" x 8"
   8 squares, 3" x 3"
2 squares, 5⅞" x 5⅞"; cut each square in half diagonally *once*
   to yield 4 triangles

From medium-green print #1, cut:
2 squares, 5⅞" x 5⅞"; cut each square in half diagonally *once*
   to yield 4 triangles
4 squares, 3⅜" x 3⅜"; cut each square in half diagonally *once*
   to yield 8 triangles

From dark-pink print #1, cut:
12 squares, 3⅜" x 3⅜"; cut each square in half diagonally *once*
   to yield 24 triangles
4 strips, 2½" x 42" (binding)

Continued on page 11.

Finished quilt size: 30½" x 30½"
Finished block size: 12½" x 12½"

Designed, pieced, and machine appliquéd by Laurie Baker.
Machine quilted by Sherrie Coppenbarger.

From medium-pink print #1, cut:
10 squares, 3⅜" x 3⅜"; cut each square in half diagonally *once* to yield 20 triangles

From the *bias* of the dark-green print, cut:
Enough 1"-wide strips to equal 20" when joined end to end using straight, not diagonal, seams

From the remainder of the dark-green print, cut:
4 leaf appliqués using pattern A

From medium-green print #2, cut:
4 leaf appliqués using pattern A

From *each* of the scraps of medium-pink print #2 and dark-pink print #2, cut:
2 using the yo-yo pattern (combined total of 4)

PIECING THE BLOCKS

Sew all pieces with right sides together using a ¼" seam allowance unless otherwise noted.

1. Using the 5⅞" triangles, join a pale-yellow triangle to a medium-green #1 triangle along the long bias edges. Press the seam allowances toward the green print. Trim away the dog-ear points. Repeat for a total of four large half-square-triangle units measuring 5½" square, including seam allowances.

Make 4.

2. Repeat step 1 to sew each dark-pink, medium-pink, and medium-green 3⅜" triangle to a pale-yellow triangle to make small half-square-triangle units measuring 3" square, including seam allowances. Press the seam allowances toward the pink and green prints. Trim away the dog-ear points.

Make 24.   Make 20.   Make 8.

3. Arrange four dark-pink units, five medium-pink units, one small medium-green unit, and two pale-yellow 3" squares into three rows as shown above right. Join the pieces in each row. Press the seam allowances as indicated. Join the rows. Press the seam allowances open. Add a pale-yellow rectangle to the right side of this

unit. Press the seam allowances toward the rectangle. Repeat to make a total of four units.

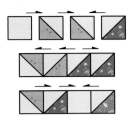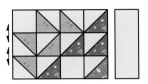

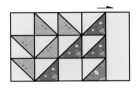

Make 4.

4. Arrange two dark-pink units and one small medium-green unit into one row as shown. Sew the units together. Press the seam allowances as indicated. Add a pale-yellow rectangle to the bottom of this unit. Press the seam allowances toward the rectangle. Join a large medium-green half-square-triangle unit to the right side of this unit. Press the seam allowances open. Repeat to make a total of four units.

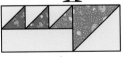

Make 4.

5. Join each unit from step 3 to a unit from step 4 to complete four blocks measuring 13" square, including the seam allowances. Press the seam allowances open.

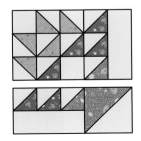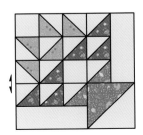

Make 4.

PIECING AND APPLIQUÉING THE QUILT TOP

1. Arrange the blocks into two rows of two blocks each as shown. Join the blocks in each row. Press the seam allowances open. Join the rows. Press the seam allowances open. The pieced quilt top should now measure 30½" x 30½", including the seam allowances.

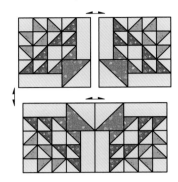

2. Refer to "Making Bias-Tube Stems and Vines" on page 90 to prepare the 1"-wide bias strip for the vine.

3. Trace the wreath guide on page 13 onto freezer paper and cut it out. Fold the guide in half vertically and then horizontally, finger-pressing the creases. With the waxy side down, align the guide creases with the seams on the right side of the quilt center; use a hot, dry iron to carefully fuse it in place. Dot the seam of the prepared vine with liquid glue and press it onto the background exactly along the guide edge, starting and stopping at a seam; trim away any excess length. Remove the wreath guide and appliqué the vine in place.

4. Using the quilt photo on page 10 as a guide, position, baste, and stitch the prepared leaf appliqués around the inside edge of the vine, positioning one end of each pair of leaves so they meet at the seam line. Remove the paper pattern pieces.

5. Select a yo-yo fabric circle. With the wrong side up, turn a portion of the edge toward you a scant ¼" to create a hem. Using a knotted length of perle cotton and the embroidery needle, bring the needle up through the hem from the wrong side of the folded fabric to bury the knot between the layers. Sew a running stitch through all of the layers, near the folded edge. Continue turning the hem to the wrong side and stitching as you work your way around the circle to your starting point; gently pull the threaded needle to gather the yo-yo edges into the center. Insert the needle under the gathered edge, just to the side of the center opening, and bring it out on the back of the yo-yo. Knot and clip the thread from the back,

keeping the gathers taut. Repeat to make a total of four yo-yos.

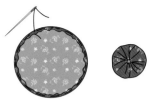

6. Place a yo-yo over the ends of a pair of leaves where they meet at the seams. Position a button over the yo-yo center and stitch through all layers using matching thread.

ADDING THE BORDER

Join a pale-yellow 3" x 25½" strip to the right and left sides of the quilt center. Press the seam allowances toward the border. Join a pale-yellow 3" x 30½" strip to the remaining sides of the quilt center. Press the seam allowances toward the border.

Quilt assembly

COMPLETING THE QUILT

Refer to "Finishing Techniques" on page 93 for details as needed. Layer the quilt top, batting, and backing. Quilt the layers. The center of the featured quilt was machine quilted with a slightly curved line that worked its way from the space between one flower's leaves to the next adjacent set of leaves. This pattern was worked around the circle and then two more lines echoed the design. The basket bottoms were quilted with a crosshatch design using a serpentine stitch, and a large flower and leaves were stitched into the lower portion of the basket. The sides of the pink basket pieces that were not touched by the flower were quilted with a curved line. The remainder of the background was stitched with a leaf-and-curlicue design. Join the four 2½" x 42" strips of dark-pink print #1 into one length and use it to bind the quilt.

Santa Fe Soup

My quilting friend Ann served this hearty soup for lunch one day when she had a bunch of friends over to sew. It was an immediate hit and we all left with full bellies and the recipe. For variety, substitute a pound of browned ground beef for the chicken or leave the meat out entirely and go vegetarian. It's delicious any way you make it! My family likes to crush up a handful of corn chips and put them in the bottom of the bowl before ladling the soup into it, and then we top it all with sour cream and cheddar cheese. ~Laurie

2 cans (11 ounces) white corn with juice
2 cans (15 ounces) black beans with juice
2 cans (14 ounces) petite diced tomatoes with juice
1 jar (16 ounces) mild salsa
1 packet (1 ounce) dry ranch dressing
2 packets (1.25 ounces) taco seasoning
2 cups shredded rotisserie chicken

Combine all ingredients in a slow cooker and mix well. Cook on high for 4 to 6 hours.

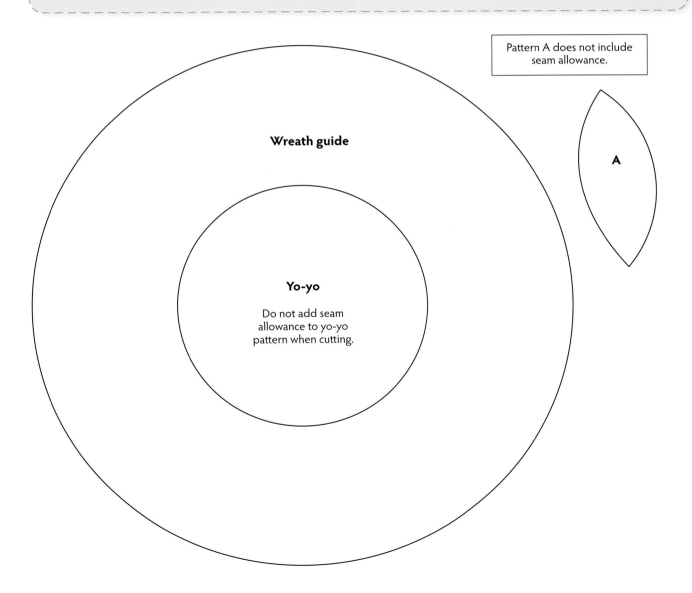

Pattern A does not include seam allowance.

Wreath guide

Yo-yo

Do not add seam allowance to yo-yo pattern when cutting.

A

easy peasy

Reminiscent of the blocks found in one of your grandmother's "everyday" quilts, these old-fashioned Churn Dash blocks boast a serving of modern style as they seem to float above a field of scrappy plaid. Show off your own personal flair as you piece this modern take on a tried-and-true classic block.

MATERIALS
15 fat quarters (18" x 22") of assorted prints for setting squares
2⅝ yards of black print for Churn Dash blocks, border, and binding
1⅞ yards of cream print for Churn Dash blocks
1⅛ yards of dark-tan print for plaid patchwork
1 fat eighth (9" x 22") of cranberry print for plaid center squares
5¼ yards of fabric for backing
79" x 93" rectangle of batting

CUTTING
Cut all pieces across the width of the fabric unless otherwise noted.

From the cream print, cut:
12 strips, 4" x 42"
3 strips, 3⅞" x 42"; crosscut into 30 squares, 3⅞" x 3⅞". Cut each
    square in half diagonally *once* to yield 60 triangles.

From the dark-tan print, cut:
24 strips, 1½" x 42"; crosscut *18 of the strips* into:
    60 rectangles, 1½" x 7"
    30 rectangles, 1½" x 4"
    Reserve the remaining 6 strips for the strip-set patchwork.

From the black print, cut:
24 strips, 2½" x 42"; crosscut *15 of the strips* into 60 rectangles,
    2½" x 8½". Reserve the remaining 9 strips for the binding.
3 strips, 3⅞" x 42"; crosscut into 30 squares, 3⅞" x 3⅞". Cut each
    square in half diagonally *once* to yield 60 triangles.
8 strips, 1½" x 42"

From the *length* of the cranberry print fat eighth, cut:
3 strips, 1½" x 22"; crosscut into 30 squares, 1½" x 1½"

From *each* of the assorted print fat quarters, cut:
4 squares, 7" x 7" (combined total of 60)

Finished quilt size: 72½" x 86½"
Finished block size: 14½" x 14½"

Designed and pieced by Kim Diehl. Machine quilted by Deborah Poole.

PIECING THE CHURN DASH BLOCKS

Sew all pieces with right sides together using a ¼" seam allowance unless otherwise noted.

1. Join a cream print 4" x 42" strip to each long edge of a dark-tan print 1½" x 42" strip. Press the seam allowances toward the dark-tan print. Repeat for a total of six strip sets. Crosscut the strip sets into 30 segments, 4" wide, and 60 segments, 1½" wide.

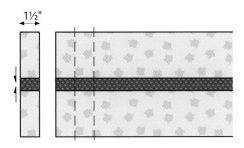

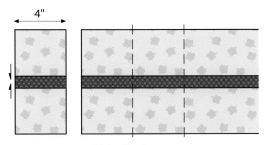

Make 6 strip sets.
Cut 30 segments, 4" wide,
and 60 segments, 1½" wide.

2. Join a cream print 3⅞" triangle and a black print 3⅞" triangle along the long bias edges. Press the seam allowances toward the black print. Trim away the dog-ear points. Repeat for a total of 60 half-square-triangle units measuring 3½" square, including the seam allowances.

Make 60.

3. Join a small strip-set segment from step 1 to a black print 2½" x 8½" rectangle as shown. Press the seam allowances toward the black print. Repeat for a total of 60 pieced units.

Make 60.

4. Join a half-square-triangle unit from step 2 to each end of a pieced unit from step 3 as shown. Press the seam allowances toward the pieced unit. Repeat for a total of 30 pieced Churn Dash units. Reserve the remaining pieced units.

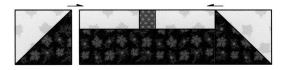

Make 30.

5. Join a dark-tan print 1½" x 4" rectangle to opposite sides of a cranberry print 1½" square. Press the seam allowances toward the dark-tan print. Repeat for a total of 15 pieced dark-tan strips.

Make 15.

6. Join a large strip-set segment from step 1 to each long side of a pieced dark-tan strip from step 5. Press the seam allowances toward the dark-tan strip. Repeat for a total of 15 pieced block center units.

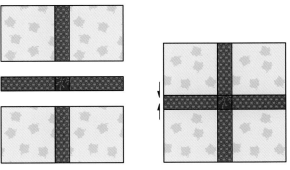

Make 15.

7. Join a reserved pieced unit from step 4 to opposite sides of a pieced block center unit. Press the seam allowances toward the black print. Repeat for a total of 15 pieced center block rows.

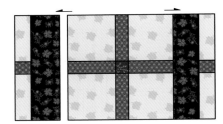

Make 15.

8. Lay out two pieced Churn Dash units from step 4 and a pieced center block row from step 7 to form a Churn Dash block. Join the rows. Press the seam allowances toward the center row. Repeat for a total of 15 Churn Dash blocks measuring 14½" square, including the seam allowances.

Make 15.

PIECING THE SETTING SQUARES

1. Join an assorted print 7" square to opposite sides of a dark-tan print 1½" x 7" rectangle. Press the seam allowances toward the dark-tan print. Repeat for a total of 30 pieced setting square units.

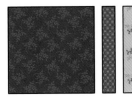

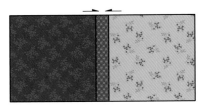

Make 30.

2. Join a dark-tan print 1½" x 7" rectangle to opposite sides of a cranberry print 1½" square. Press the seam allowances toward the dark-tan print. Repeat for a total of 15 pieced dark-tan strips.

Make 15.

3. Lay out two pieced setting square units from step 1 and one pieced dark-tan strip from step 2 in three horizontal rows as shown. Join the rows. Press the seam allowances toward the dark-tan strip. Repeat for a total of 15 pieced setting squares measuring 14½", including the seam allowances.

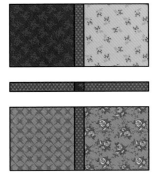 

Make 15.

PIECING THE QUILT CENTER

1. Lay out three Churn Dash blocks and two pieced setting squares in alternating positions as shown. Join the pieces to form row A. Press the seam allowances toward the setting squares. Repeat to make a total of three A rows.

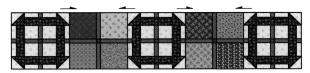

Row A. Make 3.

2. In the same manner, lay out three pieced setting squares and two Churn Dash blocks. Join the pieces to form row B. Press the seam allowances toward the setting squares. Repeat to make a total of three B rows.

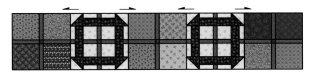

Row B. Make 3.

3. Lay out the A and B rows in alternating positions to form the quilt center. Join the rows. Press the seam allowances toward the B rows. The pieced quilt center should measure 70½" x 84½", including the seam allowances.

ADDING THE BORDER

1. Join two black print 1½" x 42" strips end to end to form a pieced border strip. Press the seam allowances to one side. Repeat for a total of four pieced border strips.

2. Fold the longest side of the quilt center in half to find the center. Align the center seam of a pieced border strip with the midpoint of the quilt center; pin the strip in place, working from the center outward to each end. Stitch the pinned border strip in place. Press the seam allowances toward the border strip. Repeat with the remaining long side of the quilt center. Trim away the excess border lengths so the strips are flush with the top and bottom edges of the quilt center.

3. Repeat step 2 with the remaining sides of the quilt center. The pieced quilt top should now measure 72½" x 86½", including the seam allowances.

COMPLETING THE QUILT

Refer to "Finishing Techniques" on page 93 for details as needed. Layer the quilt top, batting, and backing. Quilt the layers. The featured quilt was machine quilted in a swirling pattern as described in "Machine Quilting" on page 94. Join the nine black print 2½" x 42" strips into one length and use it to bind the quilt.

Peppered Bacon and Clam Chowder

I've always been a fan of soups and chowders, especially when I can simmer them in a slow cooker and enjoy their savory aromas while I'm working in my sewing room. Serve this hearty chowder with toasted English muffins or a loaf of crusty bread and dinner is done! ~Kim

6 slices peppered bacon, cut into ½" pieces
1 medium onion, peeled and diced
1 celery stalk, thinly sliced
5 medium potatoes (Yukon Golds are my favorites!), peeled and cut into a large dice
4 cans (6.5 ounces) minced clams, including juice
1 can (15 ounces) whole kernel corn, drained
3 cups low-sodium chicken broth
2 teaspoons salt (or to taste)
¼ teaspoon ground pepper
2 cups fat-free half-and-half
4 rounded tablespoons cornstarch
½ teaspoon dried parsley

Sauté the bacon, onion, and celery in a skillet over medium-high heat until golden brown (about 10 minutes); drain fat. Transfer the mixture to a large slow cooker and stir in the potatoes, clams, corn, chicken broth, salt, and pepper. Cover and cook on low for 5½ to 6 hours, until potatoes are tender. (For quicker cooking time, adjust the heat setting to high and cook for 3 hours.) Whisk together the half-and-half and cornstarch; pour into the mixture in the slow cooker, stirring gently to blend well. Add parsley. Continue cooking on the high setting, uncovered, for 30 minutes or until the chowder is warmed through and thickened.

When life has you running in circles, escape to your quilting corner and let your cares melt into your stitches. Before you know it, you'll be feeling relaxed and you'll have a finished quilt top to show for the time you've taken to treat yourself.

MATERIALS
1¾ yards of tan print for block backgrounds and border
½ yard of red print for blocks and border
½ yard of teal print for blocks and border
¼ yard of teal-striped fabric for blocks
½ yard of coordinating tan print for binding
3⅓ yards of fabric for backing
55" x 55" square of batting

CUTTING
Cut all pieces across the width of the fabric unless otherwise noted.

From the tan print, cut:
3 strips, 6½" x 42"; crosscut into 16 squares, 6½" x 6½"
2 strips, 4½" x 42"
11 strips, 2½" x 42"; crosscut 4 of the strips into 8 strips, 2½" x 18½"

From the red print, cut:
6 strips, 2½" x 42"; crosscut 2 of the strips into:
    16 squares, 2½" x 2½"
    4 rectangles, 2½" x 4½"

From the teal print, cut:
5 strips, 2½" x 42"; crosscut 1 of the strips into:
    4 rectangles, 2½" x 4½"
    4 squares, 2½" x 2½"

From the teal-striped fabric, cut:
2 strips, 2½" x 42"; crosscut into 20 squares, 2½" x 2½"

From the coordinating tan print, cut:
6 strips, 2½" x 42" (binding)

Finished quilt size: 48½" x 48½"
Finished block size: 22" x 22"

Designed and pieced by Laurie Baker. Machine quilted by Sherrie Coppenbarger.

PIECING THE BLOCKS

Sew all pieces with right sides together using a ¼" seam allowance unless otherwise noted.

1. Join one tan print 4½" x 42" strip, one red print 2½" x 42" strip, and one tan print 2½" x 42" strip as shown to make a strip set. Press the seam allowances toward the red strip. Crosscut the strip set into 16 segments, 2½" wide.

Make 1 strip set.
Cut 16 segments.

2. Join two tan print and two red print 2½" x 42" strips as shown to make a strip set. Press the seam allowances toward the red strips. Crosscut the strip set into 16 segments, 2½" wide.

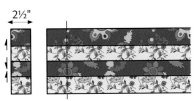

Make 1 strip set.
Cut 16 segments.

3. Lay out two segments from step 1 and two segments from step 2 in four vertical rows as shown. Join the rows. Press the seam allowances as indicated. Repeat to make a total of eight red units.

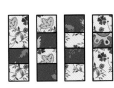

Make 8.

4. Repeat steps 1 and 2, substituting the teal print strips for the red print strips. Lay out two teal segments from step 1 and two teal segments from step 2 in four vertical rows as shown. Join the rows. Press the seam allowances as indicated. Repeat to make a total of eight teal units.

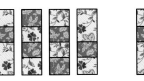

Make 8.

5. Join one red print, one tan print, and one teal print 2½" x 42" strip as shown to make a strip set. Press the seam allowances toward the red and teal strips. Crosscut the strip set into 16 segments, 2½" wide.

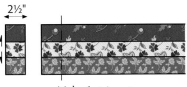

Make 1 strip set.
Cut 16 segments.

6. Sew a segment from step 5 to the top edge of each tan print 6½" square, orienting eight of the segments with the teal square on the left and the remaining eight segments with the red square on the left. Press the seam allowances as indicated.

Make 8.   Make 8.

7. Lay out five teal-striped 2½" squares and four red 2½" squares into three horizontal rows as shown, paying attention to the direction of the stripes. Sew the squares in each row together. Press the seam allowances toward the red squares. Join the rows. Press the seam allowances toward the middle row. Repeat to make a total of four center units.

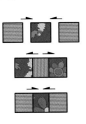

Make 4.

8. Lay out two units from step 3, two units from step 4, two of each of the units from step 6, and one unit from step 7 in three horizontal rows as shown. Pay careful attention to the direction of the stripes in the center unit. Sew the units in each row together. Press the seam allowances as indicated. Join the rows. Press the seam allowances toward the top and bottom rows. Repeat to make a total of four blocks measuring 22½" x 22½", including the seam allowances.

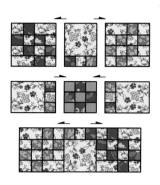
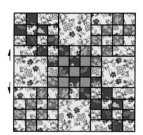

Make 4.

ASSEMBLING THE QUILT TOP

1. Lay out the blocks in two rows of two blocks each, rotating the blocks to form the pattern. Join the blocks in each row. Press the seam allowances in opposite directions. Join the rows. Press the seam allowances open. The pieced quilt center should measure 44½" square, including the seam allowances.

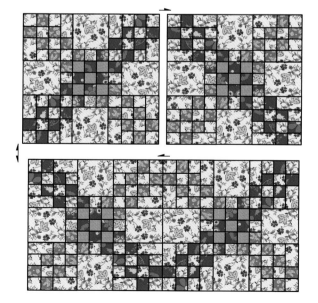

2. Join a tan print 2½" x 18½" strip to opposite ends of a red print 2½" x 4½" rectangle. Press the seam allowances as indicated. Add a teal print 2½" square to each end of the strip. Press the seam allowances as indicated. Repeat to make a total of two border strips. Refer to the quilt assembly diagram on page 25 to sew the strips to the right and left sides of the quilt center. Press the seam allowances toward the borders.

Side border.
Make 2.

3. Join a tan print 2½" x 18½" strip to opposite ends of a red print 2½" x 4½" rectangle. Press the seam allowances as indicated. Add a teal print 2½" x 4½" rectangle to each end of the strip. Press the seam allowances as indicated. Repeat to make a total of two border strips. Sew the strips to the remaining sides of the quilt center. Press the seam allowances toward the borders. The finished quilt top should now measure 48½" square, including the seam allowances.

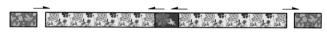

Top/bottom border.
Make 2.

COMPLETING THE QUILT

Refer to "Finishing Techniques" on page 93 for details as needed. Layer the quilt top, backing, and batting. Quilt the layers. The featured quilt was machine quilted with an allover swirl design in the background areas as well as the striped squares. The teal and red squares were stitched with a design of a "tipsy" square, in which the line on each side curves at one end and tapers to the opposite end. Join the six 2½" x 42" strips of coordinating tan print into one length and use it to bind the quilt.

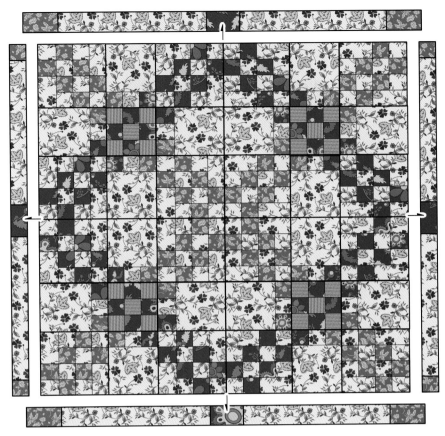

Quilt assembly

Chicken Tostadas

Spice up mealtime with this Mexican-inspired dish. You can make the flavor more pungent simply by using a hotter picante sauce, but be careful—cooking the chicken in the sauce intensifies the heat. The chicken is equally good for tacos or enchiladas. ~Laurie

4 skinless, boneless chicken breasts (about 2 pounds), cut into chunks
1 jar (16 ounces) mild picante sauce
10 tostada shells
1 can (16 ounces) refried beans
2 tablespoons water
Shredded cheese, lettuce, tomato, guacamole, onions, and sour cream (optional)

Place the chicken in the slow cooker and cover with the picante sauce. Cook on low 4 to 6 hours or until the chicken shreds easily. Pour the chicken mixture into a strainer to eliminate the liquid but retain the larger chunks of picante sauce. Return the mixture to the slow cooker and use two forks to shred the chicken.

Follow the package instructions to warm the tostada shells in the oven. Meanwhile, heat the refried beans and 2 tablespoons of water in a small saucepan until warmed through and spreadable; add more water if necessary. Spread each tostada shell with refried beans, and then top with the shredded chicken mixture. Garnish with cheese, lettuce, tomato, guacamole, onions, and sour cream if desired.

blackbirds and berries

Break out your favorite scraps and charm squares, and whip up this sweet little wall hanging in no time at all. With its sprinkling of juicy berries and plump blackbirds, this colorful quilt can be tucked into the smallest niche of your home for some everblooming charm.

MATERIALS

1 fat quarter (18" x 22") of medium-tan print for patchwork border
1 rectangle, 12½" x 16½", of light-tan print for center block
28 squares, 2½" x 2½", of assorted prints for patchwork border.
   (To reduce the number of prints needed, select 14 assorted print charm squares, 5" x 5"; from each square, cut two squares, 2½" x 2½", to yield a combined total of 28 squares.)
28 squares, 1½" x 1½", of assorted prints for patchwork border.
   (To reduce the number of prints needed, cut 14 assorted print rectangles, 1½" x 3"; crosscut each rectangle in half to yield a combined total of 28 squares, 1½" x 1½".)
4 squares, 3½" x 3½", of assorted prints for border corner posts
1 fat quarter of black print for blackbird appliqués and binding
1 chubby sixteenth (9" x 11") of medium-green print for stem, large leaf, and calyx appliqués
1 rectangle, 5" x 10", of light-green print for large leaf top and small leaf appliqués
1 rectangle, 3" x 10", of brown print for vase appliqué
1 rectangle, 5" x 9", of red print for large trumpet flower and berry appliqués
1 rectangle, 3" x 5", of gold print for small trumpet flower appliqué
1 square, 4½" x 4½", of coordinating red print for round flower appliqué
1 square, 5" x 5", of pink print for round flower middle and berry appliqués
1 square, 2" x 2", of dark-blue print for round flower center appliqué
3 rectangles, 2" x 4", of assorted red prints for berry appliqués
¾ yard of fabric for backing
25" x 29" rectangle of batting
Bias bar
Liquid basting glue for fabric

Finished quilt size: 18½" x 22½"

Designed, pieced, machine appliquéd, and hand quilted by Kim Diehl.

CUTTING

Cut all pieces across the width of the fabric unless otherwise noted. Refer to "Cutting Bias Strips" on page 86 to cut bias strips. For greater ease, appliqué preparation instructions are provided separately below.

From the *length* of the medium-tan print fat quarter, cut:
4 strips, 3½" x 22"; crosscut into:
    10 rectangles, 3½" x 4½"
    8 rectangles, 2½" x 3½"

From the *length* of the black print fat quarter, cut:
5 strips, 2½" x 22" (binding)
Reserve the remaining black print for the appliqués.

From the *bias* of the medium-green print chubby sixteenth, cut:
1 strip, 1¼" x 10"
2 strips, 1¼" x 6"
Reserve the remaining medium-green print for appliqués.

PREPARING THE APPLIQUÉS

Refer to pages 32 and 33 for appliqué patterns A–L.

1. Using the quilt photo on page 28 as a guide, and referring to "Materials" on page 26 and "Kim's Invisible Machine Appliqué Technique" beginning on page 87, prepare the following:

    + 1 large trumpet flower appliqué using pattern A
    + 1 small trumpet flower appliqué using pattern B
    + 1 calyx appliqué using pattern C
    + 1 large leaf top appliqué and 1 large reversed leaf top appliqué using pattern D
    + 1 large leaf appliqué and 1 large reversed leaf appliqué using pattern E
    + 1 round flower appliqué using pattern F
    + 1 round flower middle appliqué using pattern G
    + 1 round flower center appliqué using pattern H
    + 1 vase appliqué using pattern I*
    + 1 blackbird appliqué and 1 reversed blackbird appliqué using pattern J
    + 4 small leaf appliqués using pattern K
    + 12 berry appliqués using pattern L

    * *To easily prepare the vase pattern piece, cut a rectangle of freezer paper approximately 3" x 10". Fold the rectangle in half and finger-press a center crease. Unfold the paper and line up the crease with the dashed line of the pattern; trace the shape onto the dull side of the freezer paper. Refold the paper, anchor the layers with a pin, and cut out the shape. Unfold the paper to yield one complete vase pattern piece.*

2. Referring to "Making Bias-Tube Stems and Vines" on page 90, prepare the medium-green 1¼" x 10" and 1¼" x 6" stems.

APPLIQUÉING THE QUILT CENTER

1. Fold the light-tan 12½" x 16½" rectangle in half vertically, and use a hot dry iron to lightly press a center crease. Fold the prepared A trumpet flower and I vase appliqués in half vertically and finger-press them to mark the center positions with a crease.

2. Align the crease of the trumpet flower with the crease of the block background, positioning the top edge of the flower approximately ½" down from the top edge of the light-tan rectangle; pin in place. In the same manner, position and pin the prepared vase, placing the bottom edge approximately ½" up from the bottom edge of the light-tan rectangle.

3. Dot the crease of the light-tan background with liquid glue at approximately ½" to 1" intervals. Position the prepared 10" stem over the glue dots, centering the stem over the crease and tucking the raw ends under the flower and vase appliqués.

4. Using the quilt photo as a guide, lay out the D and E large leaf pieces, overlapping the top and bottom portions approximately ¼", and tucking the raw ends under the center stem. Pin in place.

5. Lay out the remaining appliqués and the prepared 6" stems to ensure everything fits and is to your liking. Please note that it isn't necessary to tuck the ends of the 6" stems under the center stem; simply position them in a manner that is pleasing to you with the ends under the F flower. Leaving the center stem in place, remove all but the D portion of the large leaf appliqués and the 6" stems; pin or baste these pieces to the background, and stitch them in place. Referring to "Removing Paper Pattern Pieces" on page 93, remove the paper pattern pieces from the leaves. Reposition, baste, and stitch the remaining E portions of the large leaf appliqués; remove the paper pattern pieces. Stitch the center stem in place.

6. Continue working from the bottom layer to the top to stitch the remaining appliqués to the background, remembering to remove the paper pattern pieces before adding each new layer.

PIECING AND
ADDING THE BORDER

Sew all pieces with right sides together using a ¼" seam allowance unless otherwise noted.

1. Use a pencil and an acrylic ruler to draw a diagonal line on the wrong side of each assorted print 2½" and 1½" square.

2. Layer a prepared 2½" square onto one corner of a medium-tan print 3½" x 4½" rectangle. Sew the pair together on the drawn line. Referring to "Pressing Triangle Units" on page 87, press and then trim away the layers beneath the top triangle, leaving a ¼" seam allowance. Repeat with the adjacent corner of the rectangle to form a mirror-image triangle.

3. Referring to step 2, stitch, press, and trim a prepared assorted print 1½" square to each remaining corner of the rectangle unit.

4. Repeat steps 2 and 3 to make a total of 10 large rectangle units.

5. Referring to step 2, stitch, press, and trim a prepared assorted print 2½" and 1½" square to the ends of a medium-tan print 2½" x 3½" rectangle as shown. Repeat to make a total of four small rectangle units and four small mirror-image rectangle units.

Make 4 each.

6. Sew together three large rectangle units. Press the seam allowances open. Join a small rectangle unit to each end of the sewn strip. Press the seam allowances open. Repeat for a total of two pieced strips. Referring to the quilt assembly diagram below, join these strips to the right and left sides of the quilt center. Carefully press the seam allowances toward the quilt center, taking care not to apply heat to the appliqués.

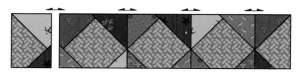

Make 2.

7. Referring to step 6, join and press two large rectangle units, two small rectangle units, and two assorted print 3½" squares. Repeat for a total of two pieced strips. Join these strips to the remaining sides of the quilt center. Press the seam allowances toward the quilt center. The pieced quilt top should now measure 18½" x 22½", including the seam allowances.

Quilt assembly

COMPLETING THE QUILT

Refer to "Finishing Techniques" on page 93 for details as needed. Layer the quilt top, batting, and backing. Quilt the layers. The hand quilting of the featured quilt used outlining of the appliqués to emphasize their shapes, plus echo quilting in the background of the quilt center. The border patchwork was stitched in the ditch (along the seam lines) with repeating straight lines in the border background areas at ½" and ¼" intervals, and double Xs were stitched onto the corner squares. Join the five black print 2½" x 22" strips into one length and use it to bind the quilt.

Chicken Pot Pie

This dish is the best when you're in the mood for a little bit of old-fashioned comfort food. To make the preparation of this recipe super fast, I buy a whole rotisserie chicken and freeze any leftover meat and bones to give me a jump on making a pot of chicken soup another day. ~Kim

1 purchased pie crust to make a 9" pie
4 tablespoons butter
6 tablespoons flour
3 cups milk (Kim uses skim)
2 tablespoons chicken bouillon granules
½ teaspoon seasoned salt
½ teaspoon lemon pepper
2 cups rotisserie chicken, shredded
1 can (8½ ounces) sliced carrots, drained
1 cup frozen baby peas
1 cup frozen pearl onions

Preheat oven to 375°. Remove the pie crust from the refrigerator and allow it to warm to room temperature while you prepare the filling. In a large saucepan, melt butter over medium-high heat. Add flour and cook about 1 minute while stirring. Pour in milk and whisk until thickened and bubbly, about 5 minutes. Stir in chicken bouillon granules, seasoned salt, and lemon pepper. Add the chicken and vegetables. Pour the filling mixture into the pie plate and top with pie crust, rolling under and crimping the edges to fit the plate. Cut three or four slits in the center of the crust. Bake 40 minutes, or until crust is golden brown. If edges of crust begin to become too brown, protect them with a folded strip of aluminum foil.

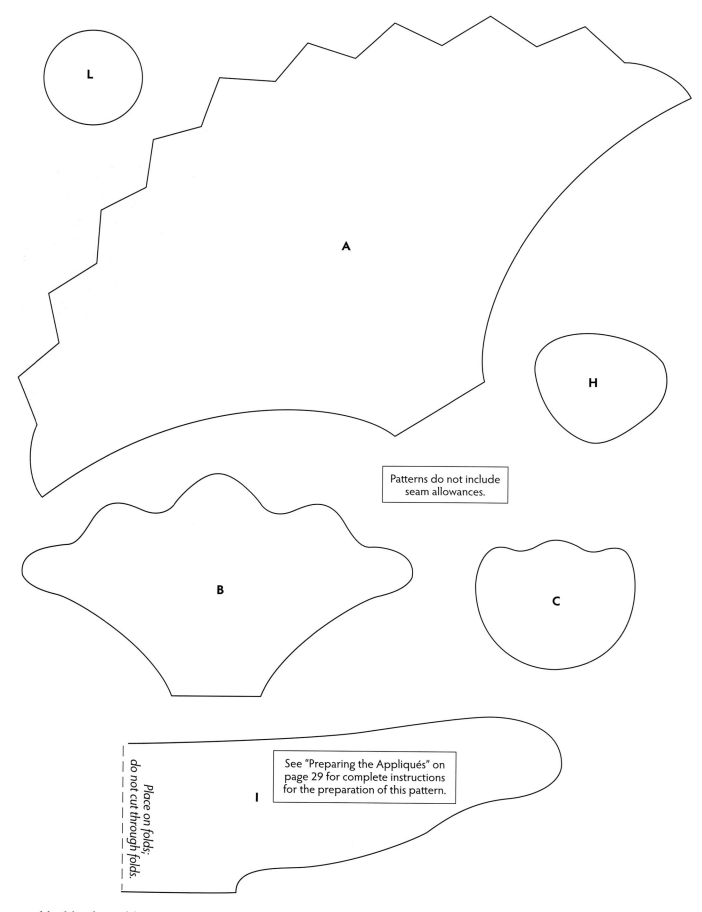

L

A

H

Patterns do not include
seam allowances.

B

C

Place on folds;
do not cut through folds.

I

See "Preparing the Appliqués" on
page 29 for complete instructions
for the preparation of this pattern.

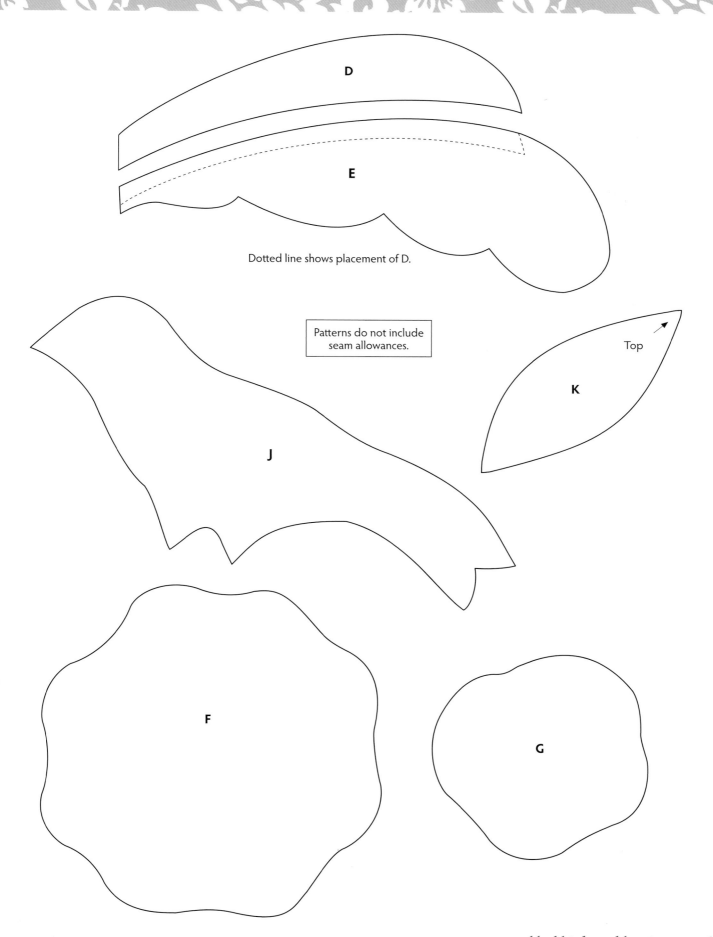

D

E

Dotted line shows placement of D.

Patterns do not include seam allowances.

K

Top

J

F

G

four patch potpourri

Dig into your scrap bag or collection of charm squares, pick your favorite prints, and then mix up a batch of simple Four Patch blocks. It's the perfect recipe for making a quilt you'll be sure to love.

MATERIALS

26 fat eighths (9" x 22") or 3¼ yards *total* of assorted medium and dark prints for medium and small circle appliqués and inner and outer border Four Patch blocks

⅝ yard *each* of 2 assorted light prints for center appliquéd block background

1 fat quarter (18" x 22") of red print for flower petal appliqués

1 fat quarter of green print for stem and leaf appliqués

3 chubby sixteenths (9" x 11") of assorted green prints for leaf appliqués

1 square, 12" x 12", of black print for large center flower appliqué

1 square, 9" x 9", of gold print for small center flower appliqué

5 charm squares (5" x 5") of assorted prints for large circle appliqués

⅝ yard of blue print for binding

4¼ yards of fabric for backing

70" x 70" square of batting

Bias bar

Liquid basting glue for fabric

CUTTING

Cut all pieces across the width of the fabric unless otherwise noted. Refer to "Cutting Bias Strips" on page 86 to cut bias strips. For greater ease, appliqué preparation instructions are provided separately on page 37.

From the *bias* of the green fat quarter for stems and leaves, cut:
4 strips, 1¼" x 15"

From *each* of the 2 assorted light prints, cut:
2 squares, 18½" x 18½" (combined total of 4)

From the assorted medium and dark prints, cut a *total* of:
80 squares, 5" x 5"
208 squares, 2¾" x 2¾"

From the blue print, cut:
7 strips, 2½" x 42" (binding)

Finished quilt size: 63½" x 63½"
Finished center block size: 36" x 36"
Finished Large Four Patch block size: 9" x 9"
Finished Small Four Patch block size: 4½" x 4½"

Designed and pieced by Laurie Baker. Appliquéd by Kim Diehl.
Machine quilted by Sherrie Coppenbarger.

PREPARING THE APPLIQUÉS

Refer to pages 39–41 for appliqué patterns A–G.

1. Using the quilt photo on page 36 as a guide and referring to "Materials" on page 34 and "Kim's Invisible Machine Appliqué Technique" beginning on page 87, prepare the following:
   * 4 flower petal appliqués using pattern A
   * 1 large flower appliqué using pattern B
   * 1 small flower appliqué using pattern C
   * 5 large circle appliqués using pattern D
   * 9 medium circle appliqués using pattern E
   * 13 small circle appliqués using pattern F
   * 24 leaf appliqués using pattern G

2. Refer to "Making Bias-Tube Stems and Vines" on page 90 to prepare the green 1¼" x 15" bias strips.

PIECING AND APPLIQUÉING THE QUILT CENTER

Sew all pieces with right sides together using a ¼" seam allowance unless otherwise noted.

1. Arrange the light 18½" squares into two rows of two squares each. Sew the squares in each row together. Press the seam allowances open. Sew the rows together. Press the seam allowances open. The pieced quilt center should measure 36½" x 36½", including the seam allowances.

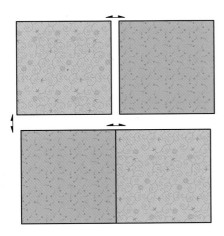

2. With right sides together, fold the center background four-patch unit from step 1 in half diagonally in both directions and lightly press the creases using a hot, dry iron. Open up the piece.

3. Fold the prepared B appliqué in half horizontally and vertically and finger-press the creases. Open the piece and align the creases with the seam lines on the right side of the background four-patch unit; pin the shape in place.

4. Referring to the quilt photo, dot the seam of each prepared 15" stem with liquid glue and press it onto a diagonal crease, tucking the raw end under the B appliqué approximately ¼". Referring to the quilt photo again, position and baste four leaves and one F appliqué along each stem. Remove the B appliqué and stitch the stems, leaves, and F appliqués in place. Remove the paper pattern pieces.

5. Fold the prepared A appliqués in half and finger-press the creases. Reposition the B appliqué on the background. Referring to the quilt photo, tuck the straight edge of the A appliqués under the B appliqué, aligning the creases with the background seam lines; baste in place. Remove the B appliqué and stitch the A appliqués in place. Remove the paper pattern pieces.

6. Reposition and baste the B appliqué in place. Position and baste a prepared D appliqué to the end of each stem, overlapping the stem ends approximately ¼". Stitch the B and D appliqués in place. Remove the paper pattern pieces.

7. Position, baste, and stitch the remaining appliqués in place, working from the bottom layer to the top and remembering to remove the paper pattern pieces before adding each new layer.

PIECING THE BLOCKS

1. Randomly select four assorted 5" squares. Lay out the squares in two rows of two squares each. Sew the squares in each row together. Press the seam allowances in opposite directions. Join the rows. Press the seam allowances in one direction. Repeat to make a total of 20 large Four Patch blocks measuring 9½" x 9½", including the seam allowances.

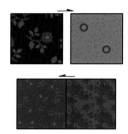
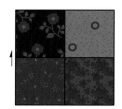

Make 20.

2. Repeat step 1 with the assorted 2¾" squares to make a total of 52 small Four Patch blocks measuring 5" x 5", including the seam allowances.

Make 52.

PIECING AND ADDING THE BORDER STRIPS

1. Stitch four large Four Patch blocks together end to end. Press the seam allowances in one direction. Repeat to make a total of two inner-border strips. Join these strips to the right and left sides of the appliquéd quilt center. Carefully press the seam allowances toward the pieced border strips, taking care not to apply heat to the appliqués. Stitch six large Four Patch blocks together end to end. Press the seam allowances in one direction. Repeat to make a total of two inner-border strips. Join these strips to the remaining sides of the appliquéd quilt center. Press the seam allowances toward the pieced border strips.

2. Stitch 12 small Four Patch blocks together end to end. Press the seam allowances in one direction. Repeat to make a total of two outer-border strips. Join these strips to the right and left sides of the quilt center, rotating the strips so that the seam allowances oppose the inner-border seam allowances. Press the seam allowances toward the outer-border strips. Stitch 14 small Four Patch blocks together end to end. Press the seam allowances in one direction. Repeat to make a total of two outer-border strips. Join these strips to the remaining sides of the quilt center, rotating the strips as before so that the seam allowances oppose. Press the seam allowances toward the outer-border strips.

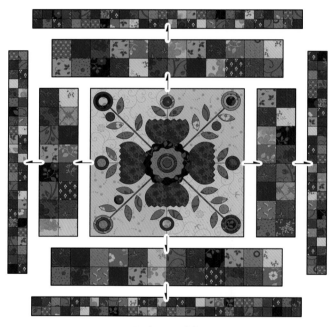

Quilt assembly

COMPLETING THE QUILT

Refer to "Finishing Techniques" on page 93 for details as needed. Layer the quilt top, batting, and backing. Quilt the layers. Each appliqué of the featured quilt was outlined stitched and then detail stitching was added to define the flower, leaf, and berry shapes. The background of the center was quilted with a swirl design, and the borders were quilted as one unit with a diagonally oriented swirl-and-curlicue design. Join the seven blue 2½" x 42" strips into one length and use it to bind the quilt.

Pizza Casserole

You don't have to be a kid to love this casserole. Add your favorite pizza toppings to the biscuit mixture and it's a guaranteed family pleaser. ~Laurie

1 pound ground Italian sausage
½ cup chopped onion
½ cup diced pepperoni
8 ounces fresh button mushrooms, sliced
1 jar (14 ounces) pizza sauce
3 tubes (7½ ounces) refrigerated
   buttermilk biscuits
2 cups shredded mozzarella cheese

Preheat oven to 350°. In a large skillet, brown the sausage and onion over medium heat; drain excess grease. Return the meat mixture to the pan and stir in the pepperoni, mushrooms, and pizza sauce. Cut each biscuit into quarters. I use my kitchen shears sprayed with cooking spray to make this easier.

Coat a 9" x 13" baking dish with cooking spray. Arrange half of the biscuits in the prepared dish. Pour half of the sauce over the biscuits and then sprinkle with half of the cheese. Repeat with the remaining biscuits, sauce, and cheese. Bake 25 to 30 minutes or until golden brown.

Patterns do not include seam allowances.

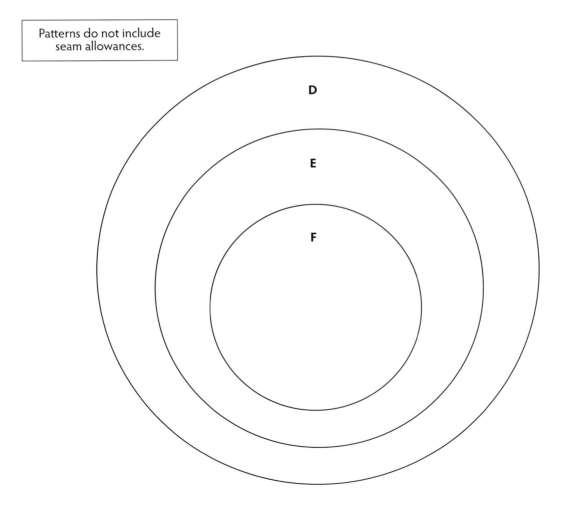

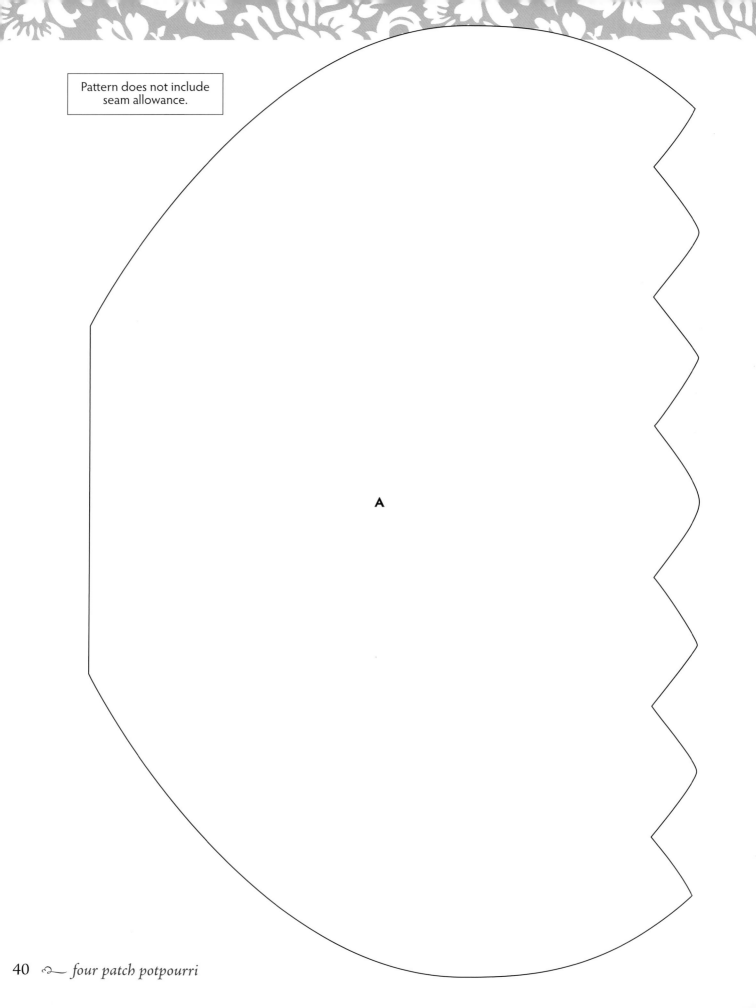

Pattern does not include
seam allowance.

A

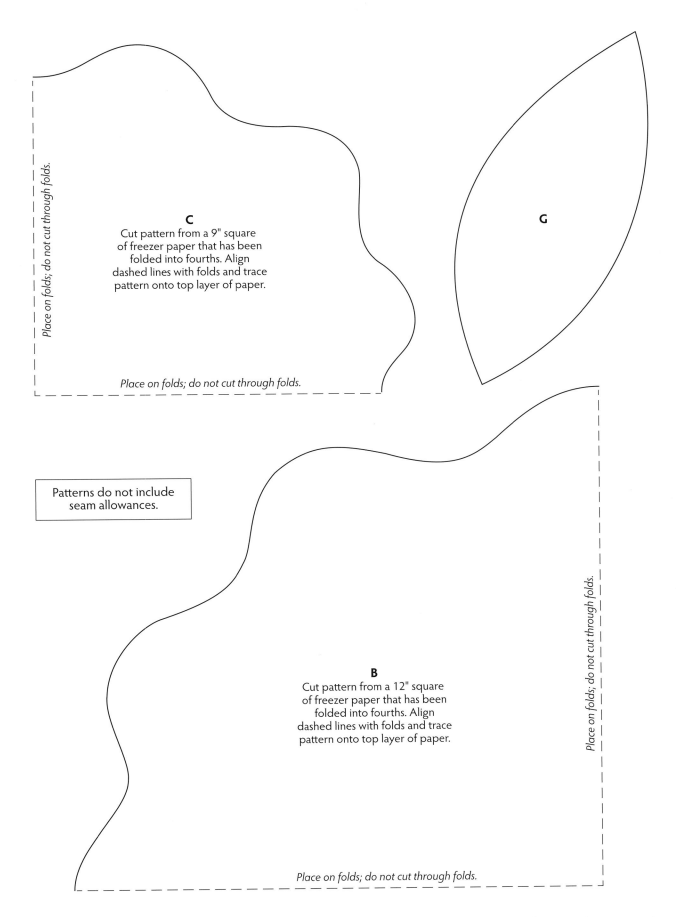

C
Cut pattern from a 9" square of freezer paper that has been folded into fourths. Align dashed lines with folds and trace pattern onto top layer of paper.

Place on folds; do not cut through folds.

Place on folds; do not cut through folds.

G

Patterns do not include seam allowances.

B
Cut pattern from a 12" square of freezer paper that has been folded into fourths. Align dashed lines with folds and trace pattern onto top layer of paper.

Place on folds; do not cut through folds.

Place on folds; do not cut through folds.

plain jane

A *new twist on traditional blocks, sparkling jewel-tone prints and an abundance of quilting stitches come together to create this lap quilt that's anything but plain. Long on style and short on sewing time, you'll want to keep this comfy quilt within easy reach.*

MATERIALS

2 yards of blue print for border

30 chubby sixteenths (9" x 11") of assorted prints for Snowball Variation blocks

4 fat quarters (18" x 22") of assorted neutral prints for Snowball Variation blocks

10 fat eighths (9" x 22") of assorted neutral prints for Rail Fence Variation blocks

33 squares, 5" x 5", of assorted prints for Rail Fence Variation blocks

3 squares, 2½" x 2½", of assorted prints for Rail Fence Variation blocks

Enough 2½"-wide assorted print strips in random lengths to equal a 288" length of binding when pieced together end to end

4¼ yards of fabric for backing

73" x 79" rectangle of batting

CUTTING

Cut all pieces across the width of the fabric unless otherwise noted.

From the *length* of *each* assorted print chubby sixteenth, cut:
2 rectangles, 3½" x 11"; crosscut into 6 squares, 3½" x 3½" (combined total of 180)

From the *length* of *each* neutral print fat quarter, cut:
6 strips, 2½" x 22"; crosscut into 45 squares, 2½" x 2½" (combined total of 180)

Using the assorted print 5" squares, cut *each* square in half to make:
2 rectangles, 2½" x 5" (combined total of 66)

From the *length* of *each* neutral print fat eighth, cut:
3 strips, 2½" x 22"; crosscut into 9 rectangles, 2½" x 6½" (combined total of 90)

From the *lengthwise grain* of the blue print, cut:
2 strips, 6½" x 60½"
2 strips, 6½" x 66½"

Finished quilt size: 66½" x 72½"
Finished block size: 6" x 6"

Designed by Kim Diehl. Pieced by Barbara Walsh and Kim Diehl.
Machine quilted by Deborah Poole.

PIECING THE SNOWBALL VARIATION BLOCKS

Sew all pieces with right sides together using a ¼" seam allowance unless otherwise noted.

1. Use a pencil and an acrylic ruler to draw a diagonal line on the wrong side of each neutral print 2½" square. Layer a prepared square over one corner of an assorted print 3½" square. Stitch the pair together on the drawn line. Referring to "Pressing Triangle Units" on page 87, press and trim the resulting corner triangle. Repeat to make a total of 180 pieced squares.

Make 180.

2. Lay out four pieced squares to make a Snowball Variation block. Join the squares in each horizontal row. Press the seam allowances in opposite directions. Join the rows. Press the seam allowances open. Repeat to make a total of 45 Snowball Variation blocks measuring 6½" square, including the seam allowances.

Make 45.

PIECING THE RAIL FENCE VARIATION BLOCKS

1. Select three assorted print 2½" x 5" rectangles. Join the rectangles along the long edges to make a strip set. Press the seam allowances toward the middle rectangle. Crosscut the strip set at the center point to make two strip-set units measuring 2½" x 6½". Repeat to make a total of 44 strip-set units.

Cut each strip set in half.
Make 44 strip-set units.

2. Select one strip-set unit and two assorted neutral print 2½" x 6½" rectangles. Join a neutral rectangle to each long edge of the unit. Press the seam allowances toward the strip-set unit. Repeat to make a total of 44 Rail Fence Variation blocks measuring 6½" square, including the seam allowances.

Make 44.

3. Sew together the three assorted print 2½" squares to make a pieced rectangle. Press the seam allowances toward the center square. Use this pieced rectangle and the two remaining neutral print rectangles to make one additional Rail Fence Variation block as instructed in step 2.

PIECING THE QUILT CENTER

When laying out the Rail Fence Variation blocks to make the pieced rows as instructed below, take care to rotate some or all of the blocks with a repeated pieced center rectangle so that the top and bottom positions are reversed. Doing this will give the illusion of using many more unique blocks and create added variety in the look of your patchwork.

1. Lay out five Snowball Variation blocks and four Rail Fence Variation blocks in alternating positions. Join the blocks to form row A. Press the seam allowances toward the Rail Fence Variation blocks. Repeat to make a total of five A rows.

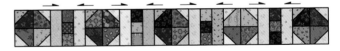

Row A.
Make 5.

2. Lay out five Rail Fence Variation blocks and four Snowball Variation blocks in alternating positions. Join the blocks to form row B. Press the seam allowances toward the Rail Fence Variation blocks. Repeat to make a total of five B rows.

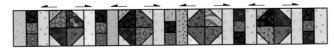

Row B.
Make 5.

3. Beginning with an A row, lay out the A and B rows in alternating positions. Join the rows. Press the seam allowances toward the B rows. The pieced quilt center should measure 54½" x 60½", including the seam allowances.

ADDING THE BORDER

Join a blue print 6½" x 60½" strip to the right and left sides of the quilt center. Press the seam allowances toward the blue print. Join the blue print 6½" x 66½" strips to the remaining sides of the quilt center. Press the seam allowances toward the blue print. The pieced quilt top should now measure 66½" x 72½", including the seam allowances.

COMPLETING THE QUILT

Refer to "Finishing Techniques" on page 93 for details as needed. Layer the quilt top, batting, and backing. Quilt the layers. The featured quilt top was machine quilted with Xs along the center row of each Rail Fence block. The Snowball Variation blocks were quilted with repeating concentric lines, and the border was quilted with a curling feather design. Join the 2½"-wide random lengths of assorted prints into one strip and use it to bind the quilt.

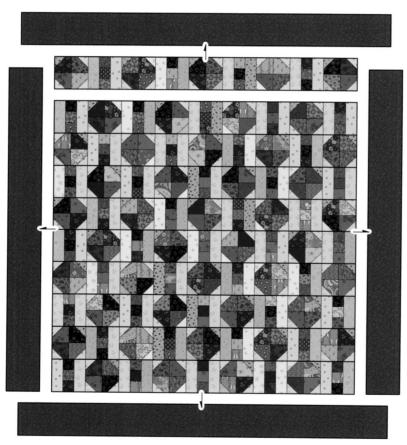

Quilt assembly

Kim's Favorite Meat Loaf

Here's a meat loaf recipe that everyone will love! If you somehow end up with leftovers, try slicing the cold loaf into 1"-thick slices, grill in an oiled skillet until warmed through, and serve on a toasted roll with provolone cheese and the condiments of your choice. ~Kim

1¼ to 1½ pounds ground turkey (or substitute lean ground beef, if you prefer)
1 cup crushed Pepperidge Farm Goldfish or other cheese crackers
½ cup cocktail sauce, plus a bit extra for topping
1 egg
¼ cup dried minced onions
1 tablespoon dried parsley flakes
1 teaspoon salt (or to taste)
1 teaspoon garlic powder
¼ teaspoon ground pepper

Preheat oven to 350° and coat a casserole dish with non-stick cooking spray. In a large mixing bowl, combine all ingredients. Shape the mixture into a loaf and place in the dish. Cover and bake 30 minutes. Spread the top of the loaf with cocktail sauce, and then bake uncovered an additional 30 to 45 minutes, until loaf is golden brown and cooked through.

Note: Here's an alternative to baking if you like the convenience of preparing meals with a slow cooker. Cut a long strip of aluminum foil and fold in half lengthwise. Line your slow cooker with this strip, extending each end of the foil beyond the rim several inches (these will serve as handles for removing the cooked loaf). Spray the prepared slow cooker with non-stick cooking spray and place the meat loaf into the pot. Cook on low 6 to 7 hours. Spread cocktail sauce over the loaf and continue cooking one additional hour, or until done.

Camping out can be fun (even if you're inside) when you sleep under the restful stars of this scrappy bed-sized quilt. All you need now is the melody of frogs and crickets singing their nighttime songs to lull you into a peaceful slumber.

MATERIALS

4⅝ yards *total* of assorted cream and tan prints for background
2½ yards of coordinating tan print for outer border
1⅝ yards *total* of assorted medium and dark prints for stars
1⅓ yards of red print for inner border and binding
5⅝ yards of fabric for backing
72" x 92" rectangle of batting

CUTTING

Cut all pieces across the width of the fabric unless otherwise noted.

From the assorted medium and dark prints, cut a *total* of:
60 squares, 3⅜" x 3⅜"; cut each square in half diagonally *once*
   to yield 120 triangles
120 squares, 3" x 3"

From the assorted cream and tan prints, cut a *total* of:
16 squares, 10½" x 10½"
8 rectangles, 5½" x 10½"
64 rectangles, 3" x 10½"
12 rectangles, 3" x 5½"

From the red print, cut:
7 strips, 3" x 42"
8 strips, 2½" x 42" (binding)

From the *lengthwise grain* of the coordinating tan print for outer border, cut:
2 strips, 3" x 80½"
2 strips, 3" x 65½"

PIECING THE BLOCKS

Sew all pieces with right sides together using a ¼" seam allowance unless otherwise noted.

1. Randomly select two medium or dark 3⅜" triangles and join them along the long bias edges. Press the seam allowances to one side. Trim away the dog-ear points. Repeat to make a total of 60 half-square-triangle units.

Make 60.

Finished quilt size: 65½" x 85½"
Finished block size: 5" x 5"

Designed and pieced by Laurie Baker. Machine quilted by Sherrie Coppenbarger.

2. Lay out four half-square-triangle units in two rows of two units each, making sure the seams are positioned as shown. Join the units in each row. Press the seam allowances in opposite directions. Join the rows. Press the seam allowances in one direction. Repeat to make a total of 15 blocks measuring 5½" square, including the seam allowances.

Make 15.

MAKING THE SASHING AND BORDER UNITS

1. Use a pencil and an acrylic ruler to draw a diagonal line on the wrong side of each medium or dark 3" square.

2. Layer a prepared square over one end of an assorted cream or tan 3" x 10½" rectangle. Stitch the pairs together on the drawn line. Press and trim as instructed in "Pressing Triangle Units" on page 87. Repeat for a total of 32 units and 32 mirror-image units.

Make 32 of each.

3. Sew one of each unit from step 2 together as shown to make a long single-point unit. Press the seam allowances in one direction. Repeat to make a total of 10 units.

Make 10.

4. Stitch, press, and trim a prepared medium or dark square to the opposite end of each of the remaining units from step 2 as shown. Sew one of each unit together to make a double-point unit. Press the seam

allowances in one direction. Repeat to make a total of 22 units.

Make 22 of each.   Make 22 total.

5. Referring to step 2, stitch, press, and trim a prepared square to each assorted cream or tan 3" x 5½" rectangle to make six short single-point units and six mirror-image units. Sew one of each unit together as shown. Press the seam allowances in one direction. Repeat to make a total of six units.

Make 6 of each.   Make 6 total.

PIECING THE QUILT CENTER

1. Lay out three blocks, two long single-point units, and two double-point units as shown to form row A. Join the pieces. Press the seam allowances open. Repeat to make a total of five A rows.

Row A.
Make 5.

2. Lay out four assorted cream or tan 10½" squares and three double-point units as shown to form row B. Join the pieces. Press the seam allowances open. Repeat to make a total of four B rows.

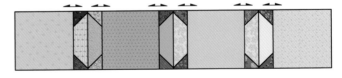

Row B.
Make 4.

3. Lay out four assorted cream or tan 5½" x 10½" rectangles and three short single-point units as shown to make row C. Join the pieces. Press the seam allowances open. Repeat to make a total of two C rows.

Row C.
Make 2.

4. Refer to the quilt assembly diagram below to lay out the A and B rows in alternating positions. Join the rows. Press the seam allowances open. Add a C row to the top and bottom edges of the pieced unit as shown. Press the seam allowances open. The pieced quilt center should measure 55½" x 75½", including the seam allowances.

ADDING THE BORDERS

1. Join the red print 3" x 42" strips end to end to make one long strip. From this pieced strip, cut two strips 75½" long and join them to the right and left sides of the quilt center. Press the seam allowances toward the border strips. From the remainder of the pieced strip, cut two strips, 60½" long, and join them to the remaining sides of the quilt center. Press the seam allowances toward the border strips.

2. Sew the tan print 3" x 80½" strips to the right and left sides of the quilt center. Press the seam allowances

toward the inner border. Join the tan print 3" x 65½" strips to the remaining sides of the quilt center. Press the seam allowances toward the inner border. The pieced quilt should now measure 65½" x 85½", including the seam allowances.

COMPLETING THE QUILT

Refer to "Finishing Techniques" on page 93 for details as needed. Layer the quilt top, batting, and backing. Quilt the layers. The featured quilt was machine quilted with feathered wreaths in the center of each star and curved lines along the outer edges of each star point. Larger feathered wreaths with crosshatched centers were quilted into the large plain squares, and another feather design was used for the sashing and outer border. A rope design was used to quilt the inner border. Join the eight red print 2½" x 42" strips into one length and use it to bind the quilt.

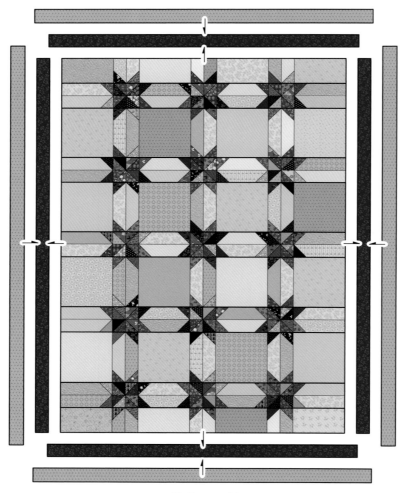

Quilt assembly

Beef Stroganoff

This rich and creamy dish is delicious enough for special occasions and easy enough for weekday dinners. Add a side salad and your meal is complete! ~Laurie

1½ to 2 pounds tenderized top round steak or sirloin steak, cut into ¼"-wide strips
8 ounces fresh button mushrooms, sliced
2 cans (10.75 ounces) condensed cream of mushroom soup
1 packet (1.8 ounces) dry onion-mushroom soup mix
½ cup beef broth
1 tablespoon Dijon mustard
¼ teaspoon paprika
½ cup sour cream
4 ounces cream cheese
1 package (8 ounces) wide egg noodles

Place the sliced meat and mushrooms in the slow cooker. In a medium bowl, mix the mushroom soup, onion-mushroom soup mix, beef broth, mustard, and paprika until blended. Pour over the meat mixture and stir to coat. Cook on low 6 to 8 hours.

About 15 to 20 minutes before serving, add the sour cream and cream cheese, stirring occasionally until blended. Meanwhile, prepare the egg noodles according to the package directions; drain. Serve the beef mixture over hot egg noodles.

farmhouse furrows

Long a favorite of quiltmakers everywhere, the humble Nine Patch block continues to wow us with its versatility. Whether you dress it up or dress it down, this simple block brings an undeniable yet quiet charm and honors our quilting heritage.

MATERIALS
14 chubby sixteenths (9" x 11") of assorted prints for Nine Patch units
18 squares, 3⅞" x 3⅞", of assorted prints for half-square-triangle units
1 yard of cream print for patchwork
⅔ yard of chocolate print for border and binding
1⅓ yards of fabric for backing
32" x 49" rectangle of batting

CUTTING
Cut all pieces across the width of the fabric unless otherwise noted.

From the *length* of *each* assorted print chubby sixteenth, cut:
3 strips, 1½" x 11" (combined total of 42). Keep the strips organized by print.

From the cream print, cut:
11 strips, 1½" x 44"; without trimming away the selvages, crosscut each strip into 4 lengths, 11" each (combined total of 44; 2 are extra).
Note: Don't worry if your fabric measures slightly less than 44" wide, as there is some "cushion" built into the strip lengths.
2 strips, 3⅞" x 42"; crosscut into 18 squares, 3⅞" x 3⅞". Cut each square in half diagonally *once* to yield 36 triangles.

Using the 18 assorted print squares, cut:
Each square in half diagonally *once* to yield a combined total of 36 triangles

From the chocolate print, cut:
2 strips, 3½" x 36½"
2 strips, 3½" x 18½"
4 strips, 2½" x 42" (binding)

Finished quilt size: 24½" x 42½"
Finished unit size: 9" x 9"

Designed and pieced by Kim Diehl. Machine quilted by Deborah Poole.

PIECING THE NINE-PATCH UNITS

Sew all pieces with right sides together using a ¼" seam allowance unless otherwise noted.

1. Select three matching assorted print 1½" x 11" strips and three cream print 1½" x 11" strips. Join a cream print strip to each long side of an assorted print strip to make strip set A. Press the seam allowances toward the assorted print. Join the remaining assorted print strips to the long sides of the cream print strip to make strip set B. Press the seam allowances toward the assorted print.

Strip set A   Strip set B

2. Repeat step 1 to make one A strip set and one B strip set from each print, keeping the A and B sets grouped by print. Make a total of 14 A and 14 B sets.

3. Select an A and B strip set sewn from one print. Crosscut the A strip set into six segments, 1½" wide. Crosscut the B strip set into three segments, 1½" wide.

Cut 6 segments.   Cut 3 segments.

4. Lay out two A segments and one B segment as shown to make a nine-patch unit. Join the rows. Press the seam allowances toward the middle row. Repeat to make a total of three pieced nine-patch A units measuring 3½" square from this print.

Nine-patch A units.
Make 3.

5. Repeat steps 3 and 4 using seven additional A and B strip sets to make a combined total of 24 pieced nine-patch A units.

6. Select an A and B strip set sewn from one print. Crosscut the A strip set into three segments, 1½" wide. Crosscut the B strip set into six segments, 1½" wide.

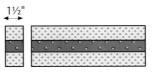 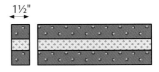

Cut 3 segments.   Cut 6 segments.

7. Lay out one A segment and two B segments as shown to make a nine-patch unit. Join the rows. Press the seam allowances away from the middle row. Repeat to make a total of three pieced nine-patch B units measuring 3½" square from this print.

Nine-patch B units.
Make 3.

8. Repeat steps 6 and 7 using five additional A and B strip sets to make a combined total of 18 pieced nine-patch B units.

PIECING THE HALF-SQUARE-TRIANGLE UNITS

Layer together an assorted print 3⅞" triangle and a cream print 3⅞" triangle. Stitch the pair together along the long bias edges. Press the seam allowances toward the assorted print. Trim away the dog-ear points. Repeat for a total of 36 pieced half-square-triangle units measuring 3½" x 3½", including the seam allowances.

Make 36.

PIECING THE QUILT CENTER

1. Referring to the illustration, lay out three nine-patch A units, two nine-patch B units, and four half-square-triangle units in three rows to form a block unit. Join the pieces in each horizontal row. Press the seam allowances away from the half-square-triangle units. Join the rows. Press the seam allowances away from the half-square-triangle units. Repeat for a total of eight pieced block units measuring 9½" square, including the seam allowances. Reserve the remaining half-square-triangle units to use in the border.
Note: You will have two extra nine-patch B units after piecing your block units; these have been included to give you added flexibility as you assemble your blocks.

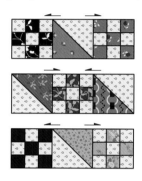
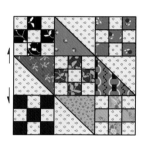

Make 8.

2. Referring to the quilt assembly diagram at right, lay out the pieced block units in four rows of two blocks each to form the quilt center. Join the block units in each row. Press the seam allowances open. Join the rows. Press the seam allowances in one direction. The pieced quilt center should measure 18½" x 36½", including the seam allowances.

ADDING THE BORDER

Join a chocolate print 3½" x 36½" strip to each long side of the quilt center. Press the seam allowances toward the chocolate print. Join a reserved half-square-triangle unit to each end of the chocolate print 3½" x 18½" strips. Press the seam allowances toward the chocolate print. Join these pieced strips to the remaining sides of the quilt center. Press the seam allowances toward the chocolate

print. The pieced quilt top should now measure 24½" x 42½", including the seam allowances.

Quilt assembly

COMPLETING THE QUILT

Refer to "Finishing Techniques" on page 93 for details as needed. Layer the quilt top, batting, and backing. Quilt the layers. The featured quilt was machine quilted in the ditch (along the seam line) of each patchwork triangle, and concentric straight lines were quilted within each triangle. An X was stitched through each nine-patch unit that fell within the X shape formed by the triangle patchwork. The center and side nine-patch units were quilted with feathered wreaths. Join the four chocolate print 2½" x 42" strips into one length and use it to bind the quilt.

extra tidbit

Finished quilt size: 20½" x 20½"

Rather than waste your leftover strip sets, make this mini nine-patch quilt as a bonus project. Cut enough 1½"-wide segments from the A and B sets to make 11 additional nine-patch units, and then add in the two extra nine-patch units remaining from step 1 of "Piecing the Quilt Center." Combine these units with 12 assorted print 3½" squares to piece together a simple quilt center, pressing the seam allowances toward the whole squares. Add simple border strips cut 3" wide and some contrasting binding for the final step . . . quick to stitch and adorable!

Slow Cooker BBQ Beef Sandwiches

My daughters love these sandwiches, especially when served with a scoop of creamy coleslaw on top. I love that I can smell the aroma of this country-style meal all through my house as it simmers away in the kitchen. ~Kim

2 cans (10¾ ounces) undiluted tomato soup
½ cup apple cider vinegar
1 cup water
2 to 3 tablespoons sugar (until you like the taste!)
1 small onion, diced
2 tablespoons Worcestershire sauce
1 teaspoon celery salt
1 teaspoon garlic powder
1 teaspoon salt
2-pound round roast (or similar type of roast), visible fat removed, cut into 2" cubes

In a large bowl, mix together all ingredients except beef; stir in cubed beef. Pour the mixture into a slow cooker and cook on low 6 to 7 hours. Pour most of the sauce into a bowl and use a potato masher to shred the beef. Add the sauce back to the slow cooker until the beef mixture is the consistency you desire, and cook another 30 minutes. Serve on split rolls or hamburger buns with chips or veggie sticks.

penny pincher

Embrace your frugal side and grab some of the larger leftover pieces from your scrap bag to make this ultra-easy throw. You'll save enough pennies to splurge on just the right print for the vertical strips that tie it all together.

MATERIALS
2⅜ yards *total* of assorted medium and dark prints for blocks
1⅜ yards of rust-red print for vertical strips and binding
3½ yards of fabric for backing
58" x 70" rectangle of batting

CUTTING
Cut all pieces across the width of the fabric unless otherwise noted.

From the assorted medium and dark prints, cut a *total* of:
75 rectangles, 3½" x 9½"
18 rectangles, 3½" x 6½"

From the rust-red print, cut:
3 strips, 9½" x 42"; crosscut into 32 rectangles, 3½" x 9½"
6 strips, 2½" x 42" (binding)

PIECING THE BLOCKS
Sew all pieces with right sides together using a ¼" seam allowance unless otherwise noted.

1. Randomly select three assorted print 3½" x 9½" rectangles and stitch them together along the long edges. Press the seam allowances in one direction. Repeat to make a total of 25 Large Strip blocks measuring 9½" x 9½", including the seam allowances.

Make 25.

2. Repeat step 1 with the assorted print 3½" x 6½" rectangles to make six Small Strip blocks measuring 6½" x 9½", including the seam allowances.

Make 6.

Finished quilt size: 51½" x 63½"
Finished Large Strip block size: 9" x 9"
Finished Small Strip block size: 3" x 6"

Designed and pieced by Laurie Baker.
Machine quilted by Sherrie Coppenbarger.

ASSEMBLING THE QUILT TOP

1. Alternately arrange five rust-red rectangles with four Large Strip blocks as shown. Join the blocks and rectangles to make row A. Press the seam allowances toward the red rectangles. Repeat to make a total of four A rows.

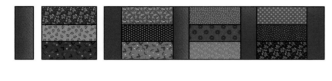

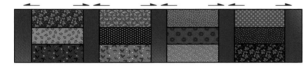

Row A.
Make 4.

2. Alternately arrange four rust-red rectangles with three Large Strip blocks. Join the blocks and rectangles to make row B. Press the seam allowances toward the red rectangles. Add a Small Strip block to each end of the strip. Press the seam allowances toward the red rectangles. Repeat to make a total of three B rows.

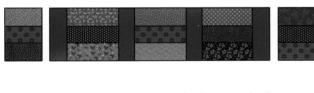

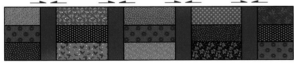

Row B.
Make 3.

3. Lay out the A and B rows in alternating positions. Join the rows. Press the seam allowances in one direction. The pieced quilt top should now measure 51½" x 63½", including the seam allowances.

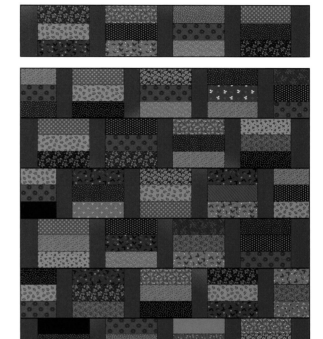

Quilt assembly

COMPLETING THE QUILT

Refer to "Finishing Techniques" on page 93 for details as needed. Layer the quilt top, backing, and batting. Quilt the layers. The featured quilt was machine quilted in an allover design of flowers and leaves. Join the six rust-red 2½" x 42" strips into one length and use it to bind the quilt.

Easy Pot Roast
This is the easiest and tastiest pot roast you'll ever make! Don't be tempted to add water to the mixture—the soups create a rich gravy that's great on mashed potatoes as well as the meat. ~Laurie

3½- to 4-pound chuck roast
1 packet (1.8 ounces) dry onion soup mix
1 can (10.75 ounces) condensed cream of mushroom soup
1 tablespoon Worcestershire sauce

Place the chuck roast in the slow cooker. In a small bowl, mix the onion soup mix, mushroom soup, and Worcestershire sauce. Pour the soup mixture over the roast. Cook on low 6 to 8 hours.

prairie star posies

Mingle warm-hued prints in a kaleidoscope of colors, a simple yet striking patchwork design, and a daisy chain of meandering appliqué shapes, and what do you get? This understated but oh-so-inviting wall quilt that's awash with star-kissed appeal.

MATERIALS

1⅛ yards of orange print for border and binding
1 yard of tan print for quilt center background
8 squares, 5⅞" x 5⅞", of assorted prints for patchwork
20 squares, 5½" x 5½", of assorted prints for patchwork, appliqués, and border corners
1 fat quarter (18" x 22") of green print for stem, leaf, and calyx appliqués
1 fat eighth (9" x 22") of orange print for flower appliqués
1 fat eighth of coordinating green print for leaf appliqués
1 chubby sixteenth (9" x 11") of wine-red print for berry appliqués
2¾ yards of fabric for backing
47" x 47" square of batting
Bias bar
Liquid basting glue for fabric
Fabric glue stick

CUTTING

Cut all pieces across the width of the fabric unless otherwise noted. Refer to page 69 for appliqué patterns A–E and to "Kim's Invisible Machine Appliqué Technique" beginning on page 87 for pattern-piece preparation. The B and C flower petal appliqués will be cut from assorted print scraps after the patchwork is complete, as instructed in "Appliquéing the Quilt Center" on page 68. Refer to "Cutting Bias Strips" on page 86 to cut bias strips.

From the tan print, cut:
1 strip, 5⅞" x 42"; crosscut into 4 squares, 5⅞" x 5⅞". Cut each square in half diagonally *once* to yield a total of 8 triangles.
4 strips, 5½" x 42"; crosscut into:
    8 rectangles, 5½" x 10½"
    8 squares, 5½" x 5½"
Note: If you're not in the habit of prewashing your fabrics, you may be able to achieve more cut pieces from each strip and reduce the number needed.

Using the assorted print 5⅞" squares, cut:
Each square in half diagonally *once* to yield a combined total of 16 triangles

From the green print fat quarter, cut:
4 *bias* strips, 1¼" x 13"
8 leaf appliqués using pattern D
4 calyx appliqués using berry pattern E

Continued on page 67.

Finished quilt size: 40½" x 40½"

Designed, pieced, and machine appliquéd by Kim Diehl.
Machine quilted by Deborah Poole.

From the coordinating green print fat eighth, cut:
16 leaf appliqués using pattern D

From the orange print fat eighth, cut:
4 flower appliqués using pattern A

From the wine-red print chubby sixteenth, cut:
12 berry appliqués using pattern E

From the orange print for border and binding, cut:
4 strips, 5½" x 30½"
5 strips, 2½" x 42" (binding)

PIECING THE QUILT CENTER

Sew all pieces with right sides together using a ¼" seam allowance unless otherwise noted.

1. Layer together two assorted print 5⅞" triangles. Stitch the pair along the long bias edges. Press the seam allowances to one side. Trim away the dog-ear points. Repeat for a total of four half-square-triangle units measuring 5½" square, including seam allowances.

Make 4.

2. Lay out the four half-square-triangle units in two rows as shown. Join the squares in each row. Press the seam allowances in opposite directions. Join the rows. Press the seam allowances open. The pieced star-center unit should measure 10½" square, including the seam allowances. Reserve the remaining assorted print 5⅞" triangles for use in step 6.

3. Use a pencil and an acrylic ruler to draw a diagonal line on the wrong side of each assorted print 5½" square.

4. Select a tan print 5½" x 10½" rectangle and two prepared assorted print squares. Layer a prepared square over one end of the tan print rectangle as shown. Stitch the pair together along the drawn line. Press and trim as instructed in "Pressing Triangle Units" on page 87. In the same manner, stitch, press, and trim a second prepared assorted print 5½" square onto the open end of the pieced rectangle, placing it in a mirror-image position. Reserve the trimmed assorted print scraps for later use. Repeat for a total of eight pieced star-point units.

Make 8.

5. Lay out the pieced star-center unit, four pieced star-point units, and four tan print 5½" squares in three horizontal rows as shown. Join the pieces in each row. Press the seam allowances of the top and bottom rows toward the tan print. Press the seam allowances of the middle row toward the star-center unit. Join the rows. Press the seam allowances away from the middle row. Reserve the remaining star-point units for use in step 7. The quilt center should measure 20½" square, including the seam allowances.

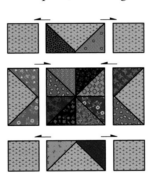 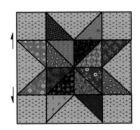

6. Layer together a reserved assorted print 5⅞" triangle and a tan print 5⅞" triangle. Stitch, press, and trim the pair as instructed in step 1. Repeat for a total of eight half-square-triangle units.

7. Join a half-square-triangle unit to each end of a reserved star-point unit as shown. Press the seam allowances toward the star-point unit. Repeat for a total of four pieced strips.

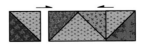

Make 4.

8. Join a pieced strip to the right and left sides of the quilt center. Press the seam allowances toward the quilt center. Join a tan print 5½" square to each end of the remaining pieced strips. Press the seam allowances toward the tan print. Join these strips to the remaining sides of the quilt center. Press the seam allowances away from the quilt center. The pieced quilt center should measure 30½" square, including the seam allowances.

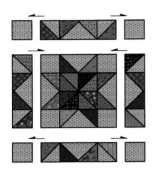 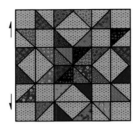

APPLIQUÉING THE QUILT CENTER

1. Referring to "Making Bias-Tube Stems and Vines" on page 90, prepare the green print 1¼" x 13" stems. For nicely finished stems, apply a small amount of fabric glue stick to one end of the wrong side of each prepared stem. Fold each glued tip under about ¼" and heat set it to anchor the fold in place.

2. Using the reserved assorted print scraps from step 4 of "Piecing the Quilt Center," prepare four B petal appliqués, four C petal appliqués, and four C reversed petal appliqués.

3. Fold a prepared A flower appliqué in half to find the center and finger-press a crease. Using the quilt photo on page 66 as a guide, lay out the prepared flower, centering it on the background by aligning the appliqué crease with the patchwork seam underneath; pin in place. Lay out a prepared 13" stem as shown, positioning the finished end farthest away from the flower and tucking any excess length underneath the flower. Pin or baste the stem in place. Lay out two green print leaves and four coordinating green print leaves, and pin or baste in place. Remove the flower appliqué and stitch the stem and leaf appliqués in place. Remove the paper pattern pieces as instructed in "Removing Paper Pattern Pieces" on page 93. Reposition, baste, and stitch the flower appliqué. Remove the paper pattern piece.

4. Continue working from the bottom layer to the top to position, baste, and stitch the remaining petal, berry, and calyx appliqués, remembering to remove the paper pattern pieces before adding each new layer. Repeat this step with each remaining side of the quilt center to complete the appliqué.

ADDING THE BORDER

Join an orange print 5½" x 30½" strip to the right and left sides of the quilt center. Press the seam allowances toward the orange print. Join an assorted print 5½" square to each end of the remaining orange print 5½" x 30½" strips. Press the seam allowances toward the orange print. Join these pieced strips to the remaining sides of the quilt center. Press the seam allowances toward the orange print. The completed quilt top should now measure 40½" square, including the seam allowances.

Quilt assembly

COMPLETING THE QUILT

Refer to "Finishing Techniques" on page 93 for details as needed. Layer the quilt top, batting, and backing. Quilt the layers. The featured quilt was machine quilted with repeating concentric lines in the center star and triangle patchwork, as well as in the ditch (along the seam lines) to define and stabilize the triangles. The appliqués were outlined for emphasis, and the tan print areas were filled with McTavishing (free-form shapes that are echo quilted inward). The borders were stitched with straight lines in wide and narrow widths to resemble bead board, and a feathered X was quilted onto each border corner square. Join the five orange print 2½" x 42" strips into one length and use it to bind the quilt.

Seafood Stuffed Tomatoes

This is a perfect no-cook dinner for a warm summer day—just add a loaf of crusty bread and some fresh fruit and you're all set! This seafood mixture also makes an excellent hors d'oeuvre spread when served in a bowl with crackers or pita chips. ~Kim

4 medium to large tomatoes, washed and cored
4 ounces light cream cheese, softened
½ cup mayonnaise
½ pound cooked lump crab meat
½ pound cooked small salad shrimp
3 green onions, sliced, including the green portions
¼ cup finely diced yellow bell pepper
¼ teaspoon salt
Lettuce leaves, dried dill weed, and lemon wedges
    for garnish

Core and cut an X into the top of each tomato, extending the cuts about halfway through the fruit. Spread the cut tomato sections slightly, and use a spoon to scoop out the seeds and pulp. Place tomatoes upside down on several thicknesses of paper towel to drain, refrigerating until ready to serve.

Use a mixer to blend the cream cheese and mayonnaise. Stir in the crab, shrimp, onions, pepper, and salt. Refrigerate at least 1 hour, until ready to serve. Use an ice-cream scoop to add the seafood mixture to each tomato. Place each stuffed tomato onto a plate lined with lettuce leaves, sprinkle with a bit of dried dill weed, and garnish with a lemon wedge.

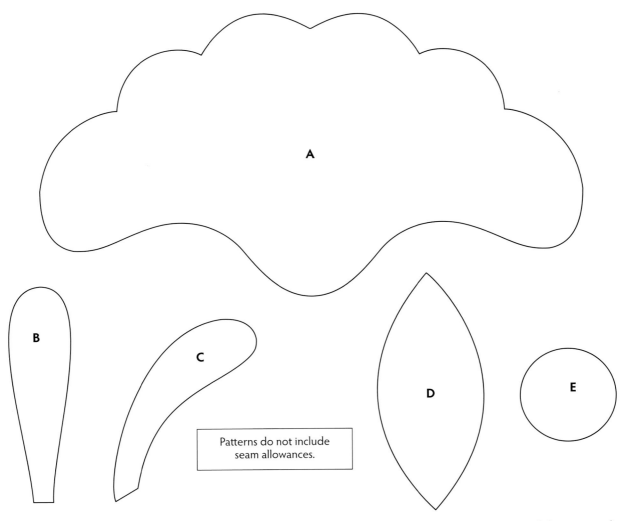

A

B

C

D

E

Patterns do not include
seam allowances.

garden ambrosia

Pick your favorite scarlet prints and sow them into a garden of sun-kissed flowers. A creamy background casts the spotlight onto the charming blocks that are sure to bring warmth to any room.

MATERIALS
5¼ yards of mottled cream fabric for blocks and pieced border
2 yards of tan solid for blocks, pieced border, and binding
⅓ yard *each* of 8 assorted light-, medium-, and dark-red prints for blocks
4½ yards of fabric for backing
77" x 77" square of batting

CUTTING
Cut all pieces across the width of the fabric unless otherwise noted.

From the mottled cream fabric, cut:
17 strips, 5½" x 42"; crosscut into 116 squares, 5½" x 5½"
25 strips, 3" x 42"; crosscut into 320 squares, 3" x 3"

From *each* of the 8 assorted red prints, cut:
16 rectangles, 3" x 5½" (combined total of 128)

From the tan solid, cut:
3 strips, 5½" x 42"; crosscut into 16 squares, 5½" x 5½"
9 strips, 3" x 42"; crosscut into 108 squares, 3" x 3"
8 strips, 2½" x 42" (binding)

PIECING THE BLOCKS
Sew all pieces with right sides together using a ¼" seam allowance unless otherwise noted.

1. Use a pencil and an acrylic ruler to lightly draw a diagonal line on the wrong side of each cream 3" square.
2. Layer a prepared cream square on opposite corners of a tan 5½" square as shown. Stitch the pairs together on the drawn lines. Trim ¼" from the stitching line and press the seam allowances toward the corners. Layer a prepared cream square over each remaining corner of the tan square as shown; stitch and trim as previously instructed. Press the seam allowances toward the center. Repeat for a total of 16 center units measuring 5½" square, including the seam allowances.

Make 16.

Finished quilt size: 70½" x 70½"
Finished Ambrosia block size: 15" x 15"
Finished Border block size: 5" x 5"

Designed and pieced by Laurie Baker. Machine quilted by Sherrie Coppenbarger.

3. Select eight matching red print 3" x 5½" rectangles. Layer a prepared cream square over one end of four rectangles as shown. Trim ¼" from the stitching line and press the seam allowances toward the corner. In the same manner, stitch, trim, and press a second prepared cream square onto the opposite end of each of these rectangles, orienting the drawn line in the same direction.

Make 4.

4. Layer a prepared cream square over one end of each of the remaining four red print rectangles as shown. Stitch the pairs together on the drawn line. Trim ¼" from the stitching line and press the seam allowances toward the rectangles. In the same manner, stitch, trim, and press a second prepared cream square onto the opposite end of each of these rectangles, orienting the drawn line in the same direction.

Make 4.

5. Stitch each rectangle from step 3 to a rectangle from step 4 as shown to make four matching block-point units measuring 5½" square, including the seam allowances. Press the seam allowances open.

Make 4.

6. Repeat steps 3–5 with the remaining red rectangles to make a total of 16 sets of block-point units. Keep matching sets of four units together.

7. Lay out one center square, four matching block-point units, and four cream 5½" squares in three rows as shown to form a block. Join the pieces in each horizontal row. Press the seam allowances open. Join the rows. Press the seam allowances open. Repeat to

make a total of 16 blocks measuring 15½" square, including the seam allowances.

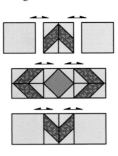 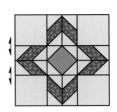

Make 16.

PIECING THE QUILT CENTER

Referring to the quilt assembly diagram on page 74, lay out the blocks in four rows of four blocks each. Join the blocks in each row. Press the seam allowances open. Join the rows. Press the seam allowances open. The pieced quilt center should measure 60½" x 60½", including the seam allowances.

PIECING AND ADDING THE BORDER

1. Use a pencil and an acrylic ruler to lightly draw a diagonal line on the wrong side of each tan 3" square.
2. Layer a prepared tan square over one corner of a cream 5½" square. Stitch the pair together on the drawn line. Trim ¼" from the stitching line and press the seam allowances toward the corner. In the same manner, stitch and trim a second prepared tan square on the adjacent corner of the cream square. Press the seam allowances toward the cream square. Repeat to make a total of 52 border blocks measuring 5½" square, including the seam allowances.

Make 52.

3. Using four of the border blocks from step 2, layer a prepared tan square over one of the remaining corners of the cream square as shown. Stitch the pairs together on the drawn line. Trim ¼" from the stitching lines and press the seam allowances toward the cream squares to make the border corner blocks.

Make 4.

4. Stitch 12 border blocks from step 2 together as shown. Press the seam allowances open. Repeat to make a total of four border strips. Stitch a border strip to the right and left sides of the quilt center. Press the seam allowances toward the border.

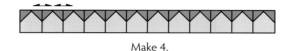

Make 4.

5. Add a border corner block to each end of the remaining two border strips. Press the seam allowances toward the border strips. Join these strips to the remaining sides of the quilt center. Press the seam allowances toward the border. The pieced quilt top should now measure 70½" square, including the seam allowances.

COMPLETING THE QUILT

Refer to "Finishing Techniques" on page 93 for details as needed. Layer the quilt top, batting, and backing. Quilt the layers. The center of each block of the featured quilt was quilted with lines in varying lengths that radiated outward and ended in a teardrop shape. The inside of each "petal" was outlined with wavy lines. A flower-and-leaf design was used to fill in the remaining background areas. Three rows of echo quilting were stitched into the dark triangles in the border. Join the eight tan 2½" x 42" strips into one length and use it to bind the quilt.

Quilt assembly

extra tidbit

Finished runner size: 6½" x 27½"

Make a bonus skinny runner by cleverly recycling your cut corners. As soon as you've accumulated a pile of trimmed-away triangle pairs, sew them together. The resulting half-square-triangle units will be all set to make another project whenever you're ready. To make this quaint little runner, select eight sets of four matching red-and-cream half-square-triangle units and 36 cream-and-tan half-square-triangle units; trim them all to 2" square. Cut four cream 2" squares. Join the matching red units to make eight Pinwheel blocks, and sew them together end to end. Sew the tan units together to make the dogtooth border, adding the cream squares at the corners. Voilà! You've got a charming accent piece to use on a dresser, table, or buffet.

❋❋❋

Stuffed Green Peppers

Even the skeptical eaters at my house love this all-in-one self-contained meal. In fact, they ate more than one pepper apiece, so if your slow cooker is large enough, you might want to double the recipe and hope you have leftovers for lunch. ~Laurie

6 green bell peppers
½ teaspoon salt plus extra for seasoning
1 pound ground round or lean ground beef
1 jar (16 ounces) thick-and-chunky salsa
½ cup uncooked long-grain rice (not instant)
2 cups shredded Cheddar cheese, divided
1 tablespoon Worcestershire sauce
½ teaspoon pepper
½ cup water
1 can (10¾ ounces) condensed tomato soup
¼ cup tomato sauce

Bring a large pot of salted water to a boil. Wash the peppers. Cut off the tops and remove the seeds. Cook peppers in boiling water for 5 minutes; drain. Lightly salt the inside of each pepper, and set aside.

In a large bowl, mix ground beef, salsa, uncooked rice, 1 cup of the cheese, Worcestershire sauce, ½ teaspoon salt, pepper, and water. Stuff the peppers two-thirds full with the beef mixture and place them in the slow cooker. In a small bowl, mix the tomato soup and tomato sauce. Pour the tomato mixture over the peppers. Cook on low 4 to 6 hours. About 20 minutes before serving, sprinkle the remaining 1 cup of cheese over the peppers; replace the lid on the slow cooker until the cheese is melted.

crossing paths

Old friends and favorite fabrics—for a quilter, the two are often one and the same! This easy quilt is just the ticket for keeping bits of some of your favorite prints close to you so you can cross paths with them any time you need a lift in your day.

MATERIALS

3 yards of gold print for blocks, setting triangles, border, and binding

1⅛ yards of light-tan print for blocks and sashing strips

18 chubby sixteenths (9" x 11") of assorted medium and dark prints for blocks and sashing squares

3¾ yards of fabric for backing

66" x 66" square of batting

CUTTING

Cut all pieces across the width of the fabric unless otherwise noted.

From the gold print, cut:

5 strips, 2⅝" x 42"; crosscut 3 *of the strips* into 13 rectangles, 2⅝" x 6⅞"

2 squares, 17" x 17"; cut in half diagonally *twice* to yield 8 side setting triangles

2 squares, 10¼" x 10¼"; cut in half diagonally *once* to yield 4 corner setting triangles

7 strips, 5" x 42"

7 strips, 2½" x 42" (binding)

From the light-tan print, cut:

13 strips, 2⅝" x 42"; crosscut 9 *of the strips* into 36 rectangles, 2⅝" x 9½"

From the assorted medium and dark prints, cut a *total* of:

26 squares, 5⅜" x 5⅜"; cut in half diagonally *once* to yield 52 triangles

24 squares, 2⅝" x 2⅝"

PIECING THE BLOCKS

Sew all pieces with right sides together using a ¼" seam allowance unless otherwise noted.

1. Join a light-tan print 2⅝" x 42" strip to each long side of a gold print 2⅝" x 42" strip to make a strip set. Press the seam allowances toward the gold strip. Repeat to make a total of two strip sets. Crosscut the strip sets into 26 segments, 2⅝" wide.

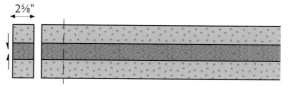

Make 2 strip sets.
Cut 26 segments.

Finished quilt size: 59¾" x 59¾"
Finished block size: 9" x 9"

Designed and pieced by Laurie Baker. Machine quilted by Sherrie Coppenbarger.

2. Sew a segment from step 1 to each long side of a gold print 2⅝" x 6⅞" rectangle. Press the seam allowances toward the gold rectangle. Repeat to make a total of 13 units.

Make 13.

3. Sew an assorted print triangle to opposite sides of a unit from step 2. Press the seam allowances toward the triangles. Sew an assorted print triangle to the remaining sides. Repeat to make a total of 13 blocks measuring 9½" square, including the seam allowances.

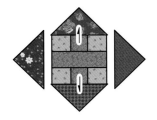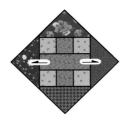

Make 13.

ASSEMBLING THE QUILT TOP

1. Lay out the blocks, light-tan sashing strips, assorted print sashing squares, and gold setting triangles in diagonal rows as shown above right. Sew the pieces in each row together, adding the corner triangles last. Press the seam allowances toward the sashing strips. Join the rows. Press the seam allowances toward the sashing rows.

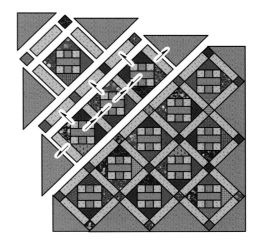

2. Join the seven gold print 5" x 42" strips end to end. Press the seam allowances to one side. From the pieced strip, cut two 50¾"-long strips and two 59¾"-long strips. Sew the 50¾"-long strips to the right and left sides of the quilt center. Press. Sew the 59¾"-long strips to the remaining sides of the quilt center. Press all seam allowances toward the border strips. The quilt top should now measure 59¾" square, including the seam allowances.

COMPLETING THE QUILT

Refer to "Finishing Techniques" on page 93 for details as needed. Layer the quilt top, batting, and backing. Quilt the layers. The featured quilt was quilted with a feather design through the gold pieces and corner triangles of the block center, and a complementary feather design in the setting triangles and border. The light tan pieces were quilted with a crosshatch design in the block and a feather design in the sashing. Join the seven gold print 2½" x 42" strips into one length and use it to bind the quilt.

Easiest Chicken Dinner Ever

There simply isn't an easier dinner than this tasty chicken dish! With its ease of preparation and simple ingredients, this is one of my "go-to" meals when I'm in the mood for comfort food without a lot of fuss. ~ Kim

3 or 4 frozen boneless and skinless chicken breast halves
Salt and pepper to taste
16 ounces sour cream (Kim uses light)
1 can (10¾ ounces) undiluted cream of mushroom soup
1 envelope dry onion soup mix
1 can (7¾ ounces) sliced mushrooms, drained

Place frozen chicken in slow cooker and lightly sprinkle with salt and pepper. Mix together sour cream, undiluted cream of mushroom soup, and dry onion soup mix; pour over chicken. Cook on low for 6 to 7 hours, until chicken is tender and cooked through. About one hour before serving, gently stir in mushrooms. If desired, garnish with parsley or snipped chives, and serve over mashed potatoes, pasta, or rice.

cozy home lane

Build your very own charming neighborhood when you piece these sweet little row houses so reminiscent of your grandmother's era. Add a sprinkling of patchwork stars for some welcoming ambience, and then embrace your inner "homebody" as you settle in for some quality quiet time.

MATERIALS
8 fat quarters (18" x 22") of assorted tan prints for patchwork blocks
6 fat quarters of assorted brown prints for House blocks and binding
24 chubby sixteenths (9" x 11") of assorted prints for House blocks
4 chubby sixteenths of assorted black prints for House blocks
6 squares, 5½" x 5½", of assorted prints for Star block center squares
48 squares, 3" x 3", of assorted prints for Star block points (scraps equivalent to approximately ¼ yard)
3¾ yards of fabric for backing
63" x 67" rectangle of batting

CUTTING
Cut all pieces across the width of the fabric unless otherwise noted.

From *each* of the assorted tan print fat quarters, cut:
2 strips, 2" x 22" (combined total of 16)
6 squares, 4½" x 4½" (combined total of 48)

From the remainder of the assorted tan print fat quarters, cut a *combined total* of:
24 squares, 3" x 3"
24 rectangles, 3" x 5½"

From *each* of the assorted brown print fat quarters, cut:
4 rectangles, 4½" x 10½" (combined total of 24)
2 strips, 2½" x 22" (combined total of 12 for binding)

From *each* of the assorted print chubby sixteenths, cut:
1 rectangle, 2½" x 10½" (combined total of 24)
2 squares, 4½" x 4½" (combined total of 48)
Keep the pieces organized by print for the House blocks.

From *each* of the assorted black print chubby sixteenths, cut:
6 rectangles, 2½" x 4½" (combined total of 24)

Finished quilt size: 56½" x 60½"
Finished block size: 10" x 10"

Designed by Kim Diehl. Pieced by Pat Peyton. Machine quilted by Deborah Poole.

PIECING THE HOUSE BLOCKS

Sew all pieces with right sides together using a ¼" seam allowance unless otherwise noted.

1. Use a pencil and an acrylic ruler to draw a diagonal line on the wrong side of each assorted tan print 4½" square.

2. Select two prepared 4½" squares from different tan prints and one assorted brown print 4½" x 10½" rectangle. Layer a tan print square over each end of the brown print rectangle as shown. Stitch the pairs together on the drawn lines. Press and trim as instructed in "Pressing Triangle Units" on page 87. Repeat for a total of 24 pieced roof units.

Make 24.

3. Select a matching set of assorted print pieces to make the base for a House block and one assorted black print 2½" x 4½" rectangle for the door. Join the 4½" assorted print house base squares to opposite long sides of the black print rectangle. Press the seam allowances toward the black print. Join the 2½" x 10½" assorted print house base rectangle to the top of the pieced door unit. Press the seam allowances toward the door unit. Repeat for a total of 24 pieced house base units measuring 6½" x 10½", including the seam allowances.

Make 24.

4. Join a pieced roof unit from step 2 to a pieced house base unit from step 3. Press the seam allowances toward the house base unit. Repeat for a total of 24 House blocks measuring 10½" square, including the seam allowances.

Make 24.

5. Lay out six House blocks to make a row. Join the blocks. Press the seam allowances open. Repeat for a total of four pieced House strips measuring 10½" x 60½", including the seam allowances.

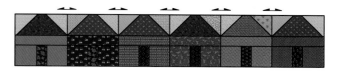

Make 4.

PIECING THE SIDEWALK UNITS

1. Select two different tan print 2" x 22" strips. Join the strips along the long sides. Press the seam allowances to one side. Repeat for a total of eight strip sets measuring 3½" x 22", including the seam allowances. Crosscut the strip sets into a total of 24 segments, 5½" wide.

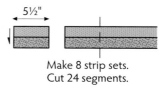

Make 8 strip sets.
Cut 24 segments.

2. Join two different strip-set segments end to end. Press the seam allowances open. Repeat for a total of 12 pieced sidewalk units.

Make 12.

3. Referring to the quilt assembly diagram on page 84, lay out six pieced sidewalk units end to end. Join the units. Press the seam allowances open. Repeat for a total of two pieced sidewalk strips measuring 3½" x 60½", including the seam allowances.

PIECING THE STAR BLOCKS

1. Use a pencil and an acrylic ruler to draw a diagonal line on the wrong side of each assorted print 3" square.

2. Select one assorted print 5½" square, eight prepared assorted print 3" squares, four assorted tan print 3" x 5½" rectangles, and four assorted tan print 3" squares. Layer a prepared assorted print 3" square over one end of a tan print 3" x 5½" rectangle. Stitch the pairs together on the drawn line. Press and trim

as instructed in "Pressing Triangle Units." Repeat for a total of four pieced rectangles. In the same manner, layer, stitch, press, and trim a second pre-pared assorted print 3" square onto the remaining end of each pieced rectangle, positioning the square to make a mirror-image point. Repeat for a total of four pieced star-point units.

Make 4.

3. Join a pieced star-point unit to opposite sides of the assorted print 5½" square. Press the seam allowances toward the center square.

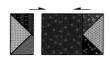

4. Join an assorted tan print 3" square to each end of the remaining star-point units. Press the seam allowances toward the tan print squares.

5. Lay out the center square unit from step 3 and the star-point units from step 4 in three horizontal rows as shown. Join the rows. Press the seam allowances open.

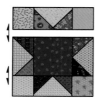

6. Repeat steps 2–5 for a total of six pieced Star blocks measuring 10½" square, including the seam allowances.

7. Lay out the Star blocks to make a row. Join the blocks. Press the seam allowances open. The pieced Star block strip should measure 10½" x 60½", including the seam allowances.

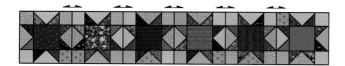

ASSEMBLING THE QUILT TOP

1. Referring to the quilt assembly diagram below, join a pieced House block strip to each long side of a pieced sidewalk strip. Press the seam allowances toward the sidewalk strip. Repeat for a total of two pieced House units.

2. Join a pieced House unit to each long side of the pieced Star block strip. Press the seam allowances away from the Star block strip. The quilt top should now measure 56½" x 60½", including the seam allowances.

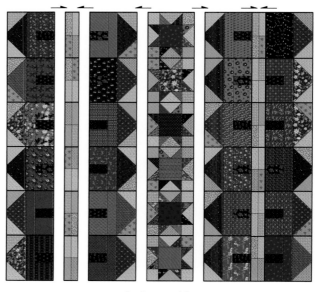

Quilt assembly

COMPLETING THE QUILT

Refer to "Finishing Techniques" on page 93 for details as needed. Layer the quilt top, batting, and backing. Quilt the layers. The featured quilt was machine quilted with a crosshatch design on the roofs, Xs in the doorways, and both vertical and horizontal lines on the houses to resemble clapboard siding, with the direction of the line alternating from house to house. An egg-and-dart design was stitched along the sidewalk patchwork, and the Star block centers were crosshatched, with triangular straight lines in the points to echo the patchwork shapes. The open sky areas were quilted with a small-scale stipple design to highlight teardrop sprays placed between the rooflines. Join the 12 assorted brown print 2½" x 22" strips into one length and use it to bind the quilt.

Rhubarb Blueberry Crisp

This yummy fruit crisp is a recipe I created to use fresh rhubarb out of my garden, and it's one of my husband's favorite desserts. Serve warm with a scoop of vanilla ice cream or a dollop of whipped cream and enjoy a little bit of home-cooked goodness! ~Kim

For the crust/topping:
1 cup flour
1 cup packed brown sugar
¾ cup quick cooking oats
½ cup (1 stick) butter, melted
1 teaspoon ground cinnamon

Place all ingredients in a medium bowl and mix until crumbly.

For the filling:
4 cups fresh rhubarb, sliced into ½"-thick pieces
1 cup fresh blueberries, washed and dried, with
   stems removed
1 cup water
1 cup sugar
2 tablespoons cornstarch
1 teaspoon vanilla extract
¼ teaspoon almond extract
¼ teaspoon salt
Enough butter to coat an 8" or 9" baking dish

Preheat oven to 350°. Butter an 8" or 9" baking dish or pie plate. Press enough of the crust/topping mixture into the bottom of the dish to make a layer about ¼" thick. Top with sliced rhubarb and sprinkle with blueberries. Add water to a small saucepan. Stir together sugar and cornstarch, and whisk into the water. Add vanilla extract, almond extract, and salt. Cook the mixture over medium heat, stirring constantly, until boiling. Remove from heat and pour over fruit. Sprinkle with the remaining crust/topping mixture. Bake uncovered 45 minutes, or until golden brown and bubbly around the edges.

quiltmaking basics

This section outlines the methods and techniques we used when making the quilts for this book. Refer to the topics included and you'll find them to be a wealth of information as you dive into your own projects. For even more details and techniques for finishing your quilts, please visit ShopMartingale.com/HowtoQuilt, where you can download free illustrated how-to information.

CUTTING BIAS STRIPS

For projects that utilize bias strips (lengths of cloth that have been cut diagonally rather than across the width of fabric), use the cutting steps provided below. This method enables you to work with a manageable size of cloth that produces strips approximately twice the cut length once they're unfolded.

1. After pressing the fabric smooth, lay it in a single layer on a large cutting mat. Grasp one corner of the fabric and fold it back to form a layered triangle of any size you choose, aligning the top straight edge with the straight grain of the bottom layer of fabric.

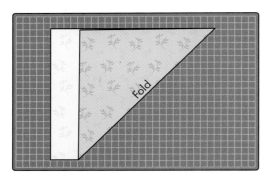

2. Rotate the layered piece of cloth, aligning the folded edge with a cutting line on your mat. (Resting an acrylic ruler over the fabric fold during this step will help ensure it's positioned in a straight line, eliminating the chance of a "dog-leg" curve in your strips after they're cut and unfolded.)

3. Use an acrylic ruler and rotary cutter to cut through the folded edge of cloth 2" to 3" from the pointed end. With the ruler lined up with the lines on the mat, begin cutting your strips at measured intervals from this edge as designated by the pattern instructions. If you reach the end of the folded edge of cloth and require additional strips, simply repeat the preceding

steps, using another corner of your cloth or squaring up the end you've been cutting.

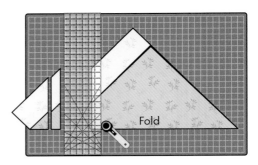

4. Square off the strip ends, trimming them to the desired length, or sew multiple lengths together to achieve the necessary length; press the seam allowances to one side, all in the same direction. If your strips will be used for bias-tube stems, using straight, *not* diagonal, seams to join multiple lengths will provide the best results, because bias bars tend to catch and become stuck on diagonal seams.

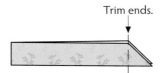

Trim ends.

PINNING

Pin your layered patchwork pieces together at regular intervals, including all sewn seams and intersections. A good tip for achieving a consistently sewn seam that extends to the back edge of your patchwork is to pin the pieces with glass-head pins; you can lay your finger over the pin heads and use the pins to steer the patchwork through the machine in a straight line, eliminating inaccurate seams at the tail end where fishtailing often occurs.

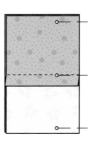

PRESSING SEAMS

Pressing well is crucial for patchwork that fits together properly. Use a hot, dry iron and the following steps when pressing your seams. Pressing *without* steam will enable you to modify your seams easily if adjustments to your patchwork become necessary.

1. Place the patchwork on a firm-surfaced ironing board with the fabric you wish to press toward (usually the darker hue) on top. On the wrong side of the fabric, briefly bring your iron down onto the sewn seam to warm the fabric.

2. Lift the iron and fold the top piece of fabric back to expose the right sides of the fabrics. While the fabric is still warm, run your fingernail along the sewn thread line to relax the fibers at the fold. Press the seam flat from the right side of the patchwork. The seam allowance will now lie under the fabric that was originally positioned on top.

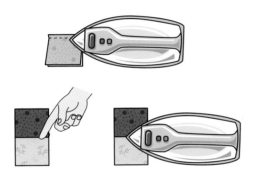

PRESSING TRIANGLE UNITS

Several projects in this book call for stitch-and-fold triangle units that are created by layering a square with a drawn diagonal line on top of a second square or rectangle. Unless otherwise instructed, after stitching the pair together on the drawn line, use the following steps.

1. Fold the top triangle back and align its corner with the corner of the bottom piece of fabric to keep it square; press in place.

2. Trim away the excess layers of fabric beneath the top triangle, leaving a ¼" seam allowance.

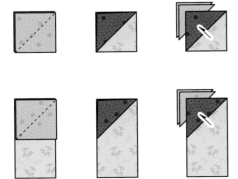

The seam allowances of triangle units are commonly trimmed *before* they are pressed, but this pressing method produces accurate patchwork that seldom requires squaring up.

KIM'S INVISIBLE MACHINE APPLIQUÉ TECHNIQUE

Laurie has been fortunate to learn Kim's technique from the master herself and now uses it for almost all of her machine-appliquéd projects. It produces a look so similar to hand appliqué that you have to look closely to tell the difference. In addition to your standard quiltmaking supplies, the following tools and products are needed for this method:

- .004 monofilament thread in smoke and clear colors
- Awl or stiletto tool with a sharp point
- Bias bars in various widths
- Embroidery scissors with a fine, sharp point
- Fabric glue stick, water-soluble and acid-free
- Freezer paper
- Iron with a sharp pressing point (travel-sized or mini appliqué irons work well for this technique)
- Liquid basting glue for fabric, water-soluble and acid-free (our favorite brand is Quilter's Choice Basting Glue by Beacon Adhesives)
- Open-toe presser foot
- Pressing board with a *firm* surface
- Sewing machine with adjustable tension control, capable of producing a tiny zigzag stitch
- Size 75/11 (or smaller) machine-quilting needles
- Tweezers with rounded tips

Choosing Your Monofilament Thread

There are currently two types of monofilament thread (sometimes called "invisible thread") available that work well for invisible machine appliqué: nylon and polyester. Both types have their own characteristics and strengths and can bring different benefits to your appliqué projects.

In our experience, nylon thread tends to produce results that are slightly less visible, but extra care should be used as your project is being assembled and pressed because this thread can be weakened by the heat of a very hot iron. For best results when working with nylon thread, avoid applying prolonged or high heat directly to the front of your appliqués, and press any nearby seams carefully. Once the project is finished and bound, the stitched appliqués will stand up well to everyday use and care. We both have had good results using the YLI brand of nylon monofilament thread.

If you'd like an extra measure of confidence that your appliqués will remain securely in place, even if they're inadvertently pressed from the front and exposed to direct heat from your iron, you may wish to use polyester monofilament thread. The look of polyester products can vary greatly from one manufacturer to another, with some appearing less transparent or even shinier than others. Depending upon the brand you choose, the monofilament thread may be slightly more visible on your stitched appliqués. For projects where we've opted to use a polyester product, we've been very pleased with the Sulky brand because the results most closely resemble those that are achieved when using nylon.

Ultimately, we recommend that you experiment with both types of monofilament thread and make this decision based upon your own personal results and preferences.

Preparing Pattern Templates

For projects featuring multiple appliqués made from one pattern, being able to trace around a sturdy template to make the number of pieces needed, rather than tracing over the pattern sheet numerous times, speeds the process tremendously and gives consistent results. Keep in mind as you make your templates that any shape can be simplified to fit your skill level. And don't be afraid to fatten up thin tips or redraw narrow inner curves to plump them—your resulting appliqués will look essentially the same, but your shapes will be much easier to work with.

To make a sturdy paper template for tracing pattern pieces, follow these steps.

1. Cut a piece of freezer paper about twice as large as your shape. Use a pencil to trace the pattern onto one end of the non-waxy side of the paper. Fold the freezer paper in half, waxy sides together, and use a hot, dry iron set on the "cotton" setting (test this setting with your own iron to make sure it isn't too hot) to fuse the folded paper layers together.

2. Cut out the shape on the drawn line, taking care to duplicate it accurately. Remember that only one template piece is needed for any shape you will be making.

Preparing Paper Pattern Pieces

Pattern pieces are used differently than pattern templates; templates are simply tools used to easily trace your shapes, while individual paper pattern pieces are what you will use as you prepare your appliqués from cloth. Always cut paper pattern pieces on the drawn

lines; you'll add the seam allowances later as you cut your shapes from fabric. To achieve smooth pattern edges, we suggest moving the paper, rather than the scissors, as you take long cutting strokes.

Use the prepared template (or pattern sheet, if you are preparing fewer than a dozen pieces) to trace the specified number of pattern pieces onto the non-waxy side of a piece of freezer paper. To save time when many pieces are required, stack the freezer paper up to six layers deep (with the waxy sides facing down) and anchor the layers together using pins in the center of the shape or staples at regular intervals about ¼" *outside* the shape in the background. Next, cut out the pattern pieces and discard the background areas.

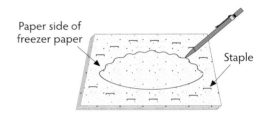

Paper side of freezer paper

Staple

Mirror-image pieces can easily be prepared by tracing the pattern onto the non-waxy side of one end of a strip of freezer paper, and then folding it accordion style in widths to fit your shape. Anchor the layers together as previously described and cut out the shape. When you separate the pieces, every other shape will be a mirror image.

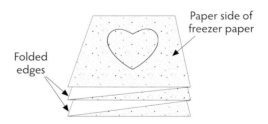

Paper side of freezer paper

Folded edges

The accordion-fold method is quick for making multiple pattern pieces of any shape that doesn't have an obvious direction, even if the shape isn't perfectly symmetrical, because this method speeds the process and adds interest to the finished quilt. Multiple pattern pieces for shapes that have an obvious direction (such as a bird) should be prepared by stacking individual freezer-paper pieces as described previously, unless a mirror-image shape is required.

Preparing Appliqués

1. Apply a small amount of glue from a fabric glue stick to the *non-waxy* side of each pattern piece and affix it

shiny side up to the wrong side of your fabric, leaving approximately ½" between each shape for seam allowances. Experience has taught us that positioning the longest lines or curves of each shape on the diagonal is best, because the resulting bias edges are easier to work with and manipulate than straight-grain edges when pressing the seam allowances over onto the paper pattern pieces.

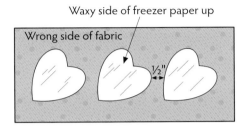

Waxy side of freezer paper up

Wrong side of fabric

½"

2. Using embroidery scissors, cut out each shape, adding an approximate ¼" seam allowance around the paper. For invisible machine appliqué, unlike traditional needle-turn appliqué, you'll find that it's actually much easier to work with seam allowances that are a bit "chubby." Keeping your seam allowances approximately ¼" in width, rather than the narrower seam allowances many of us use for needle turn, will reduce fraying and enable you to easily grab, position, and press the cloth. To help keep your seam allowances the proper width as you become comfortable cutting out your appliqués, place a piece of ¼" quilter's tape across your thumbnail (on the hand that will hold the appliqué steady as you cut it), and this will provide a perfect visual guide to help you gauge the amount to be cut!

It's easier to press and prepare the seam allowances of all outer curves and points without clipping them, but the seam allowances of inner points or pronounced inner curves should be clipped once at the center position, stopping two or three threads away from the paper and taking care not to clip into it. If you're not sure whether an inner seam-allowance curve requires a clip, try pressing it without one—if the fabric follows the shape of the curve easily, you've eliminated a step!

Clip inner points
to paper edge.

Pressing Appliqués

To prepare your appliqués for stitching, use the steps that follow to press the seam allowance of each piece, always working at the top edge of the shape (on the side that's furthest away from you). As you follow these steps, rotate the appliqué edge you are working with toward the point of your iron as you proceed around the shape in one direction from start to finish. Keep in mind that if you're right-handed, you'll want to work around the shape from right to left; if you're left-handed, simply reverse the direction. Adjust the amount of seam allowance you are working with at any given time to be in keeping with the size and curves of your appliqué. The smaller the shape or the curvier the edges, the smaller the increments should be as you rotate and press the seam allowance fabric—this will enable the fabric to smoothly conform to the shape of your appliqué and hug the paper pattern piece for flawless results. Always begin pressing along a straight edge or a gentle curve, never at a point or a corner, and rotate the appliqué toward the iron as previously instructed. This will direct the seam allowance of any points toward your "smart" hand (which will later hold the awl or stiletto to fine-tune and finish any points).

1. Beginning at a straight or gently curved edge and working your way around the entire shape, use the pad of your finger to smooth the fabric seam allowance over onto the waxy side of the paper pattern piece, following with the point of a hot, dry iron (set on the "cotton" setting) to firmly press it in place. To avoid puckered appliqué edges, always draw the seam allowance slightly back toward the last section pressed. Let the point of your iron rest on each newly pressed section of seam allowance, holding it in place as you draw the next section over onto the paper pattern piece. Allowing the iron to rest in place while you work will lengthen the amount of time the fabric receives heat, helping the cloth to fuse more firmly to the paper.

Direct seam allowance
toward center of shape.

2. For sharp outer points, press the seam allowance so the folded edge of the fabric extends beyond the first side of the pattern point, snugging the fabric firmly up against the paper edge. Fold over the seam allowance on the remaining side of the point and continue pressing. After the seam allowance of the entire piece has been pressed, apply a small amount of glue stick to the bottom of the folded flap of fabric seam allowance at the point. If the seam-allowance flap will be visible from the front of the appliqué, use the point of an awl or stiletto to drag the fabric in and away from the appliqué edge (not down from the point, as this will blunt it), and touch it with the point of a hot iron to heat set the glue and fuse it in place.

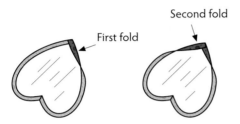

First fold

Second fold

To achieve those sharp appliqué points we all strive for, ensure that your pressed seam allowance follows the line of the curve at the point, rather than the point itself. When a point is less than perfect, it's usually because the seam allowance has flared out and away from the paper pattern piece. Following the angle of the curve leading up to each point as you press will ensure the cloth hugs the pattern piece, and the finished point will be crisp and precise.

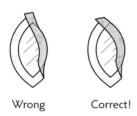

Wrong   Correct!

3. To prepare an inner point or pronounced inner curve, stop pressing the seam allowance just shy of the center clipped section. Reaching under the appliqué at the clip, use the pad of your finger to smooth the clipped section of fabric snugly onto the paper, following

immediately behind with the iron in a sweeping motion to fuse the fibers in place onto the paper.

Always turn your prepared appliqué over to the front to evaluate your pressing and adjust any areas that could be improved. Tiny imperfections can be smoothed by nudging them with the point of your hot iron, and more pronounced imperfections can be loosened and re-pressed from the back.

Making Bias-Tube Stems and Vines

To achieve finished stems and vines that can be curved flawlessly and don't require the seam allowances to be turned under, use bias tubes. After cutting the strips specified in the project instructions (and referring to "Cutting Bias Strips" on page 86 for guidelines), prepare them as follows:

1. With *wrong* sides together, fold the strip in half lengthwise and stitch a *scant* ¼" (two or three threads less than a true ¼") from the long raw edges to form a tube. For any stem sewn from a strip 1" or less in width, you may need to trim the seam allowance to approximately ⅛" so that it will be hidden when the stem is viewed from the front.

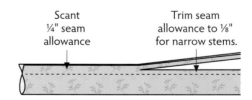

Scant ¼" seam allowance

Trim seam allowance to ⅛" for narrow stems.

2. Because of seam allowance differences that can occur, the best bias bar width for each project can vary from person to person, even for stems of the same size. Ultimately, it's best to simply choose a bar that will fit comfortably into the sewn tube, and then slide it along as you press the stem flat to one side, centering the seam allowance so it won't be visible from the front.

Bias bar

3. Remove the bias bar and place small dots of liquid basting glue at approximately 1" intervals along the seam line underneath the layers of the pressed seam allowance; use a hot, dry iron on the wrong side of the stem, allowing it to rest on each area of the stem for two or three seconds, to heat set the glue and fuse the seam allowance in place.

Basting Appliqués

Invisible machine appliqué, like traditional hand appliqué, is sewn in layers from the bottom to the top. Keep in mind as you lay out and baste your appliqués that it's a good practice to leave approximately ½" between the outermost appliqués of your design and the raw edge of your background because this will preserve an intact margin of space around each piece after the quilt top has been assembled.

1. Lay out the prepared appliqués on the background to ensure that everything fits and is to your liking. As you lay out your pieces, remember that any appliqué with a raw edge that will be overlapped by another piece (such as a stem) should be overlapped by approximately ¼" to prevent fraying.
2. Remove all but the bottom appliqués and baste them in place. Liquid basting glue is our preferred method because there are no pins to stitch around or remove and the appliqués will not shift or result in shrinkage to the background cloth as they're stitched. Glue baste your appliqués as follows:

    Without shifting the appliqué from its position, fold over one half of the shape to expose the back and place small dots of liquid basting glue along the fabric seam allowance at approximately ½" to 1" intervals. Firmly push the glue-basted portion of the appliqué in place with your hand and repeat with the remaining half of the shape. From the back, use a hot, dry iron to heat set the glue.

Preparing Your Sewing Machine

Monofilament thread produces results that are nearly invisible, and it's easy to use once you know how to prepare your sewing machine. Be sure to match your monofilament thread to your appliqué, not your background, choosing a smoke color for medium and dark prints and clear for bright colors and pastels. If you're not sure which color is best, lay a strand of each type over your print to audition them. Sometimes, especially when working with appliqués that have been prepared from medium-hued prints, you'll find that neither smoke nor clear is a perfect match. Unlike traditional needle-turn appliqué where the best choice is usually a thread color in a slightly deeper hue than your appliqué, we've found that you'll generally achieve better invisible machine appliqué results when you opt for the clear thread.

Whenever possible, use the upright spool pin position on your sewing machine for the monofilament thread, as this will produce a smooth, even feed.

1. Use a size 75/11 (or smaller) machine quilting needle in your sewing machine and thread it with monofilament.
2. Wind the bobbin with all-purpose, neutral-colored thread; a sturdy 50-weight thread works well for this technique in most sewing machines, as it will resist pulling up through the surface of your appliqués. Also, keep in mind that prewound bobbins, while convenient, can sometimes make it difficult to achieve perfectly balanced tension for this technique. *Note:* If your machine's bobbin case features a special eye for use with embroidery techniques, threading your bobbin thread through this opening will often provide additional tension control to perfectly regulate your stitches.
3. Program your sewing machine to the zigzag stitch, adjust the width and length to achieve a tiny stitch as shown below (keeping in mind that your inner stitches should land two or three threads inside your appliqué, with your outer stitches piercing the background immediately next to the appliqué), and reduce the tension setting. For many sewing machines, a width, length, and tension setting of 1 produces the perfect stitch.

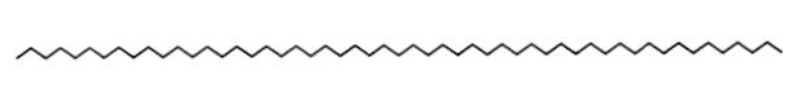

Approximate stitch size

Stitching Appliqués

Before stitching your first project with invisible machine appliqué, experiment with a simple pattern shape to become comfortable with this technique and find the best settings for your sewing machine. Keep your test piece as a quick reference for future projects, making a note directly on the background fabric as to your machine's width, length, and tension settings, and even whether your machine begins zigzag stitching on the left or the right. Also, if you routinely use more than one type of thread in your bobbin, you should make a note of the thread that was used for your test piece—if the thread in your bobbin is changed for a different type, the balance of your components may change as well, and your settings may need to be adjusted.

1. Slide the basted appliqué under the sewing-machine needle from front to back to direct the threads behind the machine, positioning a straight or gently curved edge under the needle.

2. Place your fingertip over the monofilament tail or grasp the threads as your machine takes two or three stitches. Release the thread and continue zigzag stitching around your shape, with your inner stitches landing on the appliqué and your outer stitches piercing the background immediately next to the appliqué. Train your eyes to watch the outer stitches while you sew to keep your appliqué positioned correctly, and the inner stitches will naturally fall into place. After a short distance, pause and carefully clip the monofilament tail close to the background.

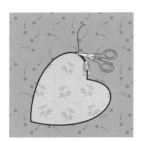

    To maintain good control, stitch each appliqué at a slow to moderate speed, stopping and pivoting as often as needed to keep the edge of your shape feeding straight toward the needle. Whenever possible, pivot with the needle down inside the appliqué, because the paper pattern piece will stabilize the shape and prevent it from stretching or becoming distorted.

    *   If dots of bobbin thread appear along the top surface edge of your appliqué as you stitch, further adjust the tension settings on your machine (usually lower) until they disappear.

    *   Your machine's stitch should look like a true zigzag pattern on the wrong side of your work. If the monofilament thread is visible underneath your appliqué from the back, or the stitches appear loose or loopy, adjust the tension settings (usually higher) until they are secure.

3. To firmly secure an inner appliqué point, stitch to the position where the inner stitch rests exactly on the inner point of the appliqué and stop. Pivot the fabric, and with the appliqué inner point at a right angle to the needle, continue stitching. For pieces with inner

points that seem delicate, pivot and stitch this area twice to secure it well.

Stop and pivot.

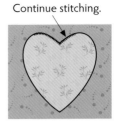
Continue stitching.

4. To secure an outer point, stitch to the position where the outer stitch lands exactly next to the appliqué point in the background and stop. Pivot the fabric and continue stitching along the next side of the shape. As you begin sewing again, a second stitch will drop into the point of the appliqué.

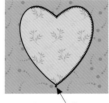
Stop and pivot.

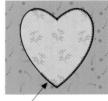
Continue stitching.

5. Continue stitching around the edge of the appliqué until you overlap your starting point by approximately ¼". End with a locking stitch if your machine offers this feature, placing it on either the appliqué or the background, wherever it will best be hidden. For machines without a locking stitch, extend your overlapped area to about ½" and your appliqué will remain well secured.

    Using a locking stitch to finish each appliqué not only makes your stitching more secure, it also communicates to your sewing machine that you've finished your current task, enabling you to easily position your next piece for stitching. As you begin stitching each new appliqué, the needle will consistently align and begin in the same position.

6. From time to time, it's a good practice to evaluate your stitch placement along your appliqué edges to ensure you're achieving the best possible results. To do this, hold a completed appliqué piece up to the light and view it with the light shining from behind. A properly stitched appliqué will have a ring of tiny needle holes encircling the appliqué in the background cloth. If your results appear different, you will need to adjust the placement of your future pieces as you stitch them.

String Appliqué

When two or more appliqués are in close proximity on the same layer, stitch your first appliqué as instructed in "Stitching Appliqués" on page 91, but instead of clipping the threads when you finish, lift the presser foot and slide the background to the next appliqué without lifting it from the sewing-machine surface. Lower the presser foot and resume stitching the next appliqué, remembering to end with a locking stitch or overlap your starting position by ¼" to ½". After the cluster of appliqués has been stitched, clip the threads between each.

Removing Paper Pattern Pieces

On the wrong side of the stitched appliqué, use embroidery scissors to carefully pinch and cut through the fabric at least ¼" inside the appliqué seam. Trim away the background fabric, leaving a generous ¼" seam allowance. Grasp the appliqué edge between the thumb and forefinger of one hand, and grab the seam allowances immediately opposite with the other hand. Give a gentle but firm tug to free the paper edge. Next, use your fingertip to loosen the glue anchoring the pattern piece to the fabric; peel away and discard the paper. Any paper that remains in the appliqué corners can be pulled out with a pair of tweezers.

Completing the Machine-Appliqué Process

Working from the bottom layer to the top, continue basting and stitching the appliqués until each one has been secured in place, remembering to remove the paper pattern pieces before adding each new layer. Keep in mind that it isn't necessary to stitch any edge that will be overlapped by another piece. If needed, *briefly* press your finished work from the back to ensure the seam allowances lie smooth and flat. Always take care not to apply direct heat to the front of your appliqués, as this could weaken the monofilament threads.

FINISHING TECHNIQUES

There are many choices available as you work through the final steps of your project—tailoring these decisions to suit your individual preferences will result in a finished quilt that's yours alone.

Batting

For quilt tops sewn from prewashed fabrics, polyester batting or a cotton/polyester blend will ensure minimal shrinkage when your quilt is laundered. If your quilt top was stitched from fabrics that weren't prewashed, choose cotton batting, particularly if you love the slightly puckered look of vintage quilts. Regardless of your choice, always follow the manufacturer's instructions for the very best results.

Backing

Cut and piece your quilt backings to be approximately 3" larger than your quilt top on all sides. As you consider your backing-fabric choices, remember that prints with a lot of texture will make your quilting less visible, while muted prints and solids will emphasize your quilting design. To prevent shadowing, use fabrics in colors similar to those in your quilt top.

For the best use of your yardage, seam your quilt backings as shown.

Lap quilts
up to 74" square

Twin-size bed quilts
up to 74" wide

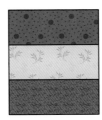
Full- and queen-size
bed quilts up to 90" wide

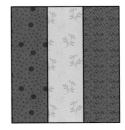
King-size bed quilts
up to 107" wide

Marking Quilting Designs

A quick and easy way to mark straight quilting lines is to use masking tape in various widths as a stitching guide, but always remember to remove the tape at the end of each day to prevent adhesive from damaging your fabric. More elaborate designs can be marked onto the top using a quilter's pencil or a fine-tipped water-soluble marker—doing this before the layers are assembled will provide a smooth marking surface and produce the best results. For a beautiful finish, always ensure your quilt features an abundant and evenly spaced amount of quilting.

Hand Quilting

To hand quilt your project, place the layered quilt top in a hoop or frame and follow these steps:

1. Thread your needle with an approximately 18" length of quilting thread and knot one end. Insert the needle into the quilt top about 1" from where you wish to begin quilting, sliding it through the layers and bringing it up through the top; gently tug until the knot is drawn down into the layer of batting.

2. Sew small, even stitches through the layers until you near the end of the thread. Make a knot in the thread about ⅛" from the quilt top. Insert and slide the needle through the batting layer, bringing it back up about 1" beyond your last stitch, tugging gently until the knot disappears; carefully clip the thread.

Hand-quilting stitch

Machine Quilting

For in-depth machine-quilting instructions, please refer to *Machine Quilting Made Easy!* by Maurine Noble (Martingale, 1994).

When an overall style of quilting is the best choice to add subtle texture without introducing another design element into the project mix, Kim's swirling pattern works well.

To stitch this versatile design, sew a free-form circle of any size, and then fill in the center with ever-reducing concentric circles (think cinnamon rolls). When you arrive at the center, stitch a gentle wavy line to the next area to be swirled and continue filling the block or quilt top, staggering the placement and size of the swirls, until the stitching is complete.

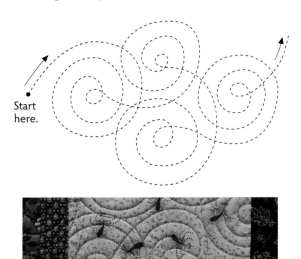

Start here.

Binding

Traditionally, a 2½"-wide French-fold binding is used to finish most quilts. When Kim binds her quilts, however, she prefers a less conventional method using 2"-wide strips that result in a traditional look from the front while producing a "chubby" border of color to frame the backing in a more striking manner. The binding yardage for each project will accommodate either method, with enough binding to encircle the quilt perimeter plus approximately 10" for mitered corners.

Traditional
French-fold binding

Chubby binding

Traditional French-Fold Binding

1. With right sides together, join the 2½"-wide strips end to end at right angles, stitching diagonally across the corners, to make one long strip. Trim the seam allowances to ¼" and press them open.

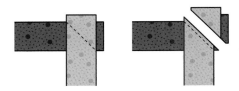

2. Cut one end at a 45° angle and press it under ¼". Fold the strip in half lengthwise with wrong sides together, and press.

Fold line

3. Beginning along one side of the quilt top, not at a corner, use a ¼" seam allowance to stitch the binding along the raw edges. Stop sewing ¼" from the first corner and backstitch. Clip the thread and remove the quilt from under the presser foot.

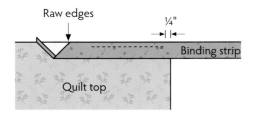

Raw edges

¼"

Binding strip

Quilt top

4. Make a fold in the binding, bringing it up and back down onto itself to square the corner. Rotate the quilt 90° and reposition it under the presser foot. Resume sewing at the top edge of the quilt, continuing around the perimeter in this manner.

5. When you approach your starting point, cut the binding end at an angle 1" longer than needed and tuck it inside the previously sewn binding to enclose the raw end. Complete the stitching.

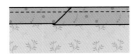

6. Bring the folded edge of the binding to the back of the quilt, enclosing the raw edges. Use a blind stitch and matching thread to hand sew the binding to the back. At each corner, fold the binding to form a miter and hand stitch it in place.

Kim's Chubby Binding

For this method, you'll need a bias-tape maker designed to produce 1"-wide, double-fold tape. For most of her quilts, Kim prefers to use binding strips that have been cut on the straight of grain, rather than the bias, because she feels this gives the quilt edges added stability. For scrappy bindings pieced from many prints of different lengths, join the strips end to end using straight seams and start with a straight fold at the beginning.

1. Cut the strips 2" wide and join them end to end. Next, slide the pieced strip through the bias-tape maker, pressing the folds with a hot, dry iron as they

emerge so that the raw edges meet in the center. As the tape maker slides along the pieced strip, the seams will automatically be directed to one side as they are pressed.

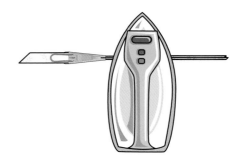

2. Open the fold of the strip along the top edge only. Turn the beginning raw end under ½" and finger-press the fold. Starting along one side of the quilt top, not at a corner, align the unfolded raw edge of the binding with the raw edge of the quilt and stitch as instructed in steps 3 and 4 of the French-fold method.

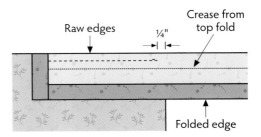

Raw edges   ¼"   Crease from top fold

Folded edge

3. When you approach your starting point, cut the end to extend 1" beyond the folded edge and complete the stitching.
4. Bring the folded edge of the binding to the back and hand stitch it (including the mitered folds at the corners) as instructed in step 6 of the French-fold method. The raw end of the strip will now be encased within the binding.

KIM DIEHL

After falling in love with a sampler quilt pattern in the late 1990s, Kim taught herself the steps needed to make it, and was forever hooked on quiltmaking. Her second quilt was of her own original design and with her third quilt, she became the winner of *American Patchwork & Quilting* magazine's 1998 Pieces of the Past quilt challenge, turning her life down a whole new and unexpected path. Kim's very favorite quilts have always been those sewn from simple tried-and-true patchwork designs, especially when combined with appliqué, and she loves designing and stitching these traditionally inspired quilts using modern techniques for the perfect blend of old and new.

Kim's work has been featured in numerous national and international quilting magazines. Her easy quilt-making and invisible machine appliqué techniques led to an extensive national teaching schedule for several years, until she retired from travel in 2011. In addition to authoring her "Simple" series of books with Martingale, Kim has designed several fabric collections for Henry Glass & Co., enabling her to be involved in the full circle of quiltmaking from start to finish—what a wonderful experience for a girl who began her journey wondering if she had what it took to make a single quilt!

LAURIE BAKER

Laurie was born itching to create something. She has scratched the surface of just about every craft genre possible, from fabric to food to furnishings, but her love of fabric remains the strongest.

While growing up, Laurie was nurtured in the needle arts by her mother, who sewed many of her clothes, and her great-aunt Kathryn, who planted the quilting seed in Laurie when she was just nine years old. Until the age of 12, Laurie lived between two elderly neighbors, Mrs. Aaron and Mrs. Graham, who introduced her to knitting, crocheting, embroidery, and many other crafts.

After graduating from college with a degree in home economics, with an emphasis in clothing and textiles, Laurie was blessed to channel that love into a career as an editor with a publisher of nationally known sewing and quilting magazines. She has spent the last 13 of her 22 years in the publishing industry as a freelance editor and writer for the quilting, sewing, and crafting industries, and she occasionally designs projects for publication.

Laurie lives in West Peoria, Illinois, with her husband, Todd; her college-aged children, Nick and Caitlin; two fat and sassy cats; and an enormous arsenal of fabric that she loves adding to. When she's not playing with needles and fabric or contemplating where to stash her latest textile acquisition, she enjoys gardening, reading, cooking, and knitting. She has no plans of entering rehab for her fabric addiction.